SHAME
OFF YOU

UNSHAMING MENTAL HEALTH STRUGGLES

Cover design: Seily Ruiz
Cover photo: Josh Fernandes
Illustrations: Teagan Fanning

ISBN: 978-0-646-99848-0

ISBN: 978-1-456-63949-5 (eBook)

10 9 8 7 6 5 4 3 2

"The two of them, the Man and his Wife, were naked, but they felt no shame."
—Genesis 2:25, *The Message*

CONTENTS

DEDICATION

This book is dedicated to all who suffer and hide silently behind the veil of shame connected with their mental health struggles. Now is the time for us to courageously come out of hiding and stand together—embracing, leveraging, and celebrating our vulnerability.

SPECIAL THANKS

To my mother Dal, and sisters, Sue, Ellie, and Annie *thank you for your positive and uplifting influence in my life. I am forever honoured to be your son and brother.*

To my wife Karen, and children, Emily and Jake *thank you for encouraging me to persevere in writing my first book. You have faithfully and lovingly stood by me, during my highest highs and my lowest lows.*

To my spiritual family, C3 Beachway and C3 Cambridge *thank you for the privilege of being your pastor for over twenty-three years and graciously accepting my flaws and weaknesses. Together we have created memories that will last a lifetime.*

NOTE TO READER

When I refer to shame, I will focus on the intimidating feeling of inferiority, or as Dr Brené Brown aptly said, "the fear that we're not good enough."

There will also be frequent references to anxiety. We all have moments when we feel anxious. As I reveal my experience, I am describing unrelenting anxiety accompanied by panic attacks. Mental health practitioners define my condition as chronic anxiety or an anxiety disorder.

SHAME OFF YOU is also a biography of the journey of my faith in God while navigating through the turmoil of shame and anxiety. Throughout this book, I make several references to vulnerability, brokenness, and weakness. My heart is to offer a fresh Biblical revelation between the relationship of taunting emotional pain and steadfast faith in God.

This book is not intended to provide medical advice or to take the place of medical advice and treatment from your General Practitioner (GP). Readers are advised to consult their GP or qualified health professionals regarding specific health and wellbeing questions.

Neither the publisher nor the author takes responsibility for possible health consequences of any person reading or following the information in this book. All readers, especially those taking prescription or over-the-counter medications, should consult their GP before beginning any exercise, nutrition or supplement program.

If you feel agitated and vulnerable while reading this book, please contact one of the organisations listed on page 173. Asking for help is a sign of courage, not weakness.

PROLOGUE

SHAME ON YOU!

It's astounding how three words can be so damaging and detrimental to the human soul. Have you ever had these three words spoken over you or perhaps you have spoken them over yourself?

We experience shame for a diversity of reasons. There may be the shame of addiction, abuse, unmanageable debt, unemployment, rejection, self-harm, chronic sickness, or moral failure. Some suffer acutely with the shame of their body image, an eating disorder, shyness, or issues with their sexuality.

Shame is not a loner. Shame has several close companions such as fear, embarrassment, humiliation, regret, and guilt. Together they stand as a formidable force on our daring road towards personal growth and maturity.

This book focuses specifically on the shame associated with our mental health struggles. Straight off the bat, I want to declare that I unashamedly belong to a gutsy tribe who suffer silently behind the veil of shame connected with chronic anxiety and panic attacks. If this is also your reality, you will identify with me on many levels.

However, if you suffer from any emotional turmoil such as unmanageable stress, burnout, depression, despair, or feeling overwhelmed, I know you too will find help and reassurance within these pages.

Telling my story is my coming out in the open. You will soon discover that I don't just have a skeleton in my closet—I have a cemetery. Shame has been a harsh voice and influence throughout my life.

From my experience, the shame associated with chronic anxiety has been intoxicating, paralysing, and intimidating. There have been dark moments when I have allowed shame to belittle and degrade me.

When my private world began to implode in early 2007, I was assigned a Mental Health Plan by my GP, and engaged in numerous challenging and confronting sessions with a therapist.

The clarifying revelation through therapy was that shame had been a constant battleground in my life—from a timid boy growing up in the western suburbs of Sydney, to my challenging role as a lead pastor of a church in Perth, Western Australia, for twenty-three years. There has been substantial collateral damage in my wake.

Scales fell off my eyes, and I could clearly see my predicament. My life had been sabotaged by a "shame double whammy." Shame was a pathway to my mental health struggle. Furthermore, if that wasn't damaging enough, my mental health struggle was a pathway to intensified and compounded shame.

Because of the perceived stigma and shame of our declining mental health, many of us desperately hide and cover up our emotional and behavioural dysfunction, just like our ancient ancestors Adam and Eve, as revealed in the Genesis narrative. They were abruptly, yet graciously exposed, and they frantically hid. Sound familiar?

Shame is a primal and painful human emotion. Today, more than any time in history, we endeavour to conceal, distract, and numb our pain of shame through medication, alcohol, shopping, social media, endless entertainment, and unrelenting busyness.

The good news is it doesn't have to be that way. As a fellow traveller of emotional brokenness, this easy-to-read, grounded, and practical book assures you that you're not alone.

Collectively, we are part of a community of the warrior wounded, learning to navigate courageously through the shame and complexities associated with our mental health struggles.

Please let me reiterate; we're in this fight together. Your pain is my pain. Your struggle is my struggle. And your breakthrough is my breakthrough.

The message of *SHAME OFF YOU* also offers unwavering hope—there is always hope and a way forward. Let me be candid right from the start. I will not be offering a silver bullet or a magical formula of recovery. There is no cookie cutter approach or a one-size-fits-all solution.

As I have battled with the turmoil of mental health struggles, I can testify that personal growth is not a quick fix, but a daring and often slow and frustrating journey that encompasses dramatic ebbs and flows. We have our good days and bad days—that's "normal," and that's okay.

Part of your reading experience will likely be a heightened self-awareness of the nature and impact of shame in your life. As you can appreciate, self-awareness is both an incredible and, at times, painful phenomenon.

To intensify your learning experience, you are invited to complete the allocated exercises in each chapter. This book is designed to be interactive—write, circle, underline, and highlight the insights and ideas that are most helpful to you.

Shame has ruthlessly strived to expose us and subsequently force us to hide. Together we prevail as *shame busters,* and together we can turn shame on its head. Now is the time to expose the true nature of shame, and force shame to hide. Now is the time to belittle and humiliate shame. Who's with me?

This book is more than typed words on a page. As you read attentively, you will hear a gentle, yet passionate voice crying out from cover to cover. There is a voice that will connect with your pain and struggle, a voice that will resonate, a voice that will offer perspective, a voice that will rattle stigmas, and false assumptions regarding our shame and mental health turmoil.

Most importantly, you will hear a calming and rhythmic sound that is seasoned with enriching grace and profound empathy. And, if you listen carefully, there is also an echo throughout every page, three potent life-giving words:

SHAME OFF YOU!

Rob Mason

shame is a voice

"Shame is the swampland of the soul."
—C. G. Jung

The ability to speak is a magnificent God-given gift we often take for granted. Through speaking, we can articulate and openly express thoughts, ideas, beliefs, convictions, doubts, solutions, dreams, and a whole range of human emotions.

As we speak, we can also tell stories, evoke a memory, ask questions, and explore new information. Ultimately the gift of speaking enables us to dialogue, engage, connect, and do life with one another.

From the soothing sound of a mother's voice towards her distraught child; to the persuasive sound of a preacher, social activist or motivational speaker; speaking can lift the human spirit to new and brilliant heights.

Shame is more than a word or noun. Shame is a voice. Shame speaks. It is possible that shame is talking to you right now. If we're not careful, we can allow shame to speak toxic words deep into our vulnerable soul. From the moment we wake up in the morning, to the time we lay our weary heads on our pillows at night, shame is shouting from the rooftops to anyone who will listen.

THE NEEDLE AND THE DAMAGE DONE

Shame is a ruthless voice, an inner critic of all things detrimental and damaging. In effect, the foundational dialect of shame is crippling condemnation. Shame rebukes and reviles. Shame is a lying and deceitful voice. Consequently, the voice of shame is notoriously venomous.

Allow me to share the first time I heard shame speak directly to me. In 1972, Canadian musician and singer-songwriter Neil Young, released the song *'The Needle and the Damage Done.'* The melodic music and raw lyrics captured the self-destruction and trauma caused by heroin addiction and overdose.

Unlike some of Neil Young's close friends, I have never been tempted to inject heroin. Nonetheless, I'm embarrassed to admit, for over twenty years I was terrified of needles.

Throughout the long night hours, I regularly experienced chilling nightmares about needles—and not just ordinary needles, but insidious and colossal needles, piercing mercilessly through my body.

Often, the night before a scheduled injection, I would be highly agitated and experienced restless sleep. In the morning, my anxiety level would shoot through the roof. I desperately wanted to run away, hide, and avoid the dreaded encounter. Where did that fear and anxiety come from?

Let me tell you a story about *the needle and the damage done.* Fear, for the most part, is a memory of danger. I can trace my irrational fear of needles and the associated acute anxiety, to a time when I was about four years old. I have a fragmented memory of my parents dropping me off at the Prince of Wales Hospital in Sydney for minor surgery under general anaesthetic.

To this day, I can still recall lying on an old metal frame bed when a nurse came and placed an aluminium foil tray on the bedside cabinet between my bed and the boy next to me. In utter horror, I saw a syringe in the foil tray. I was not naïve, even at four years old. Evidently, I had witnessed and confronted this instrument of terror earlier in my young life.

Surprisingly my first thought was, "Oh the poor boy next to me is about to have an injection." But, to my utter dismay, the nurse asked me rather abruptly, "Do you want the needle in your arm or your bottom?"

How did I respond, you might ask?

I did what any normal four-year-old boy would have done in that perilous situation—I screamed hysterically. I couldn't articulate it at the time, but in reflection, two significant and distressing issues severely damaged my innocent young soul.

First, my parents were not with me during this childhood trauma. For the first time in my life, I was vulnerable, abandoned, and utterly alone. Second, a doctor had to hold me, face down so the nurse could pull my pyjama pants down to give me an injection in my bottom. I'm not sure why I chose my bottom as the target of my affliction.

Through the humiliation of my momentary nakedness in front of a stranger and uncontrollable screaming, I believed I made a public spectacle of myself in the children's hospital ward.

Shame is a voice, and this was the first time I heard its venomous words:

You made a fool of yourself.
You're a coward.
You're weak.

The interesting feature to this distressing childhood trauma is, I don't even remember the pain of the injection. But, to this day, I vividly remember my first experience of public humiliation, coupled with intense, and paralysing fear.

The point is (pardon the pun) fear associated with needles and hospitals was ingrained in my soul at a tender and vulnerable young age. Over the coming years, I would learn the hard way that fear can be both a memory of danger and a defective learned response to a perceived threat.

More about the connection between fear and shame later in this book.

THE SHAME FILES

What has the voice of shame been saying to you recently? Can you relate to any of these false declarations that are marinated with shame?

- *You're hopeless.*
- *You're worthless.*
- *You're unlovable.*
- *You're unwanted.*
- *You're a loser.*
- *You're a coward.*
- *You're ugly.*
- *You're weak.*
- *You're clumsy.*
- *You're pathetic.*
- *You're boring.*
- *You're dumb.*
- *You're crazy.*
- *You're a fraud.*
- Other: _____

Identify the toxic thought you relate to the most. Why? _____
_____

Where did that toxic thought come from? _____
_____

How has that toxic thought impacted your life? _____
_____

From your perspective, how has that toxic thought impacted the people in your world? _____
_____

I QUIT!

Have you ever watched small children play sports? Especially with team sports like soccer, there is no game plan, set positions, or tactics. The moment the whistle or siren blows, the two opposing teams instinctively form one large mobile huddle and energetically chase the ball. This innocent and entertaining phenomenon is to the delight of the supporting family and friends standing on the sidelines cheering and laughing.

Kids' sports are all about having fun and, at times, amusingly imitating their sporting hero's antics when they kick a goal. Unfortunately, that was not my childhood experience of a team sport.

I was about six years old when I joined the Doonside Junior Soccer Club. Doonside is an unassuming suburb in the outer western suburbs of Sydney. Surrounding Doonside is the iconic blue-collar suburbs such as Blacktown and Rooty Hill. One distinguished person who attended Doonside Senior High School is V8 Supercar driver Mark 'Frosty' Winterbottom, winner of the Bathurst 1000 in 2013.

The Saturday morning soccer practice was my first experience of a team sport, and I was particularly thrilled that Dad was watching me play from the sidelines. However, because I was tentative, I stood several metres away from where all the action took place. I evidently didn't have any idea of what I was doing, but I desperately wanted to belong and for Dad to be proud of me.

I can still see the old brown leather soccer ball leaving the pack of enthusiastic boys and hurtling towards me. It must have been pure instinct, but I closed my eyes and kicked the soccer ball frantically with all my strength. Regrettably,

I also kicked the ball out of play. Then a voice from one of the boys screamed out from the pack, "Why did you kick the ball out?"

My greatest fear, even as a six-year-old boy, was the public humiliation of making a mistake and letting the team down. In my innocent mind, even at that young age, my value and significance as a person were on the line.

The jury of boys was out deliberating my self-worth. I believed, in my embryonic mind, I was exposed as incompetent and a failure. So much for kids' sports just being about fun.

THE WALK OF SHAME

I have no memory of the remainder of the soccer match. All I recall of that fateful Autumn Saturday morning was walking home slowly and despondently with Dad. After an awkward moment of silence, I told him with bitter disappointment and enflamed determination, "I quit!" For me, my walk home along Kildare Road was my walk of shame. Where did that come from?

Thinking back to my second defining moment of dysfunction, there was sadly no challenge from Dad to my reckless decision to quit the soccer team. For some unknown reason, my dad made no commitment that he would help me with my kicking skills after school or over the weekend. There was no fatherly reassurance that everything would be okay. After all, it was just a game.

My only recollection during the long walk home was Dad's silence and disengagement. My naïve childhood interpretation of Dad's tormenting silence was he must have been disappointed in me, and he too was embarrassed by my spectacular failure on the Doonside soccer field.

If you're a parent, a life lesson to glean from this incident is never underestimate the detrimental damage of silence and disengagement with your children when they experience trauma.

Allow research professor and author Dr. Brené Brown to enlighten: "Sometimes the most dangerous thing for kids is the silence *that allows them to construct their own stories*—stories that almost always cast them as alone and unworthy of love and belonging." [Braving the Wilderness, p. 15, *italics mine*]

At a young age, I was recklessly constructing my own story of apparent inferiority and worthlessness. The hideous voice of shame continued to speak and taunt me. Despondently, I continued to listen to the deceitful voice of shame. Worse still, I believed everything it was saying to me and about me.

Kicking the soccer ball out of play, fused with Dad's silence, was my second vivid memory of the shame of perceived public humiliation. That was the entry point of the primal emotion of fear and shame entering and dominating my life. This was a new chapter in my self-narrative—the story I told myself about myself.

SELF-SABOTAGE

Let's pause for a moment and allow me to reveal how subtle and sinister shame is, especially for those struggling with mental health. Shame is darker and far more lethal than similar unpleasant emotions such as embarrassment, regret, and guilt.

From my first experience of a team sport, I didn't believe I merely made a mistake by kicking the ball out of play.

My faulty conclusion was—*I am a mistake.* I didn't just fail while playing my first game of soccer—*I am a failure.* I didn't just quit the Doonside soccer team—*I am a quitter.*

What a disturbing conclusion a naïve and vulnerable six-year-old boy came to so early in life:

Rob Mason is a mistake.
Rob Mason is a failure.
Rob Mason is a quitter.

Those three negative beliefs I repeated to myself about myself was the new arsenal of subtly sabotaging my ability to engage fully in life. To self-sabotage our lives through toxic thoughts is a form of *self-harming our souls.*

Therefore, the essence of shame is intimidating, tormenting, and paralysing inferiority, to feel utterly worthless and believe you are profoundly flawed.

Welcome to *Shameville,* the dark and sinister world of shame.

ENOUGH ALREADY

Time to pause for further reflection and to enhance self-awareness. Shame is essentially feeling inferior to other people. Shame is our inner critic, a voice shouting: "You're not enough."

Which of the following "not enough" statements best capture your false beliefs about yourself?

* *I'm not good enough.*
* *I'm not smart enough.*
* *I'm not beautiful enough.*
* *I'm not good looking enough.*
* *I'm not tall enough.*
* *I'm not thin enough.*
* *I'm not strong enough.*
* *I'm not brave enough.*
* *I'm not confident enough.*
* *I'm not creative enough.*
* *I'm not worthy enough.*
* *I'm not healthy enough.*
* *I'm not wealthy enough.*
* *I'm not popular enough.*
* *I'm not assertive enough.*
* *I'm not talented enough.*
* *I'm not spiritual enough.*
* *I'm not anointed enough.*
* Or fill in the blank:
  I'm not _____ enough.

THE COMPARISON TRAP

If the essence of shame is intimidating inferiority, then at some point we have compared ourselves to other people. From afar and with envy, we gaze at other people's lifestyles, careers, houses, cars, holidays, marriages, children, and faith.

There is no doubt that social media has exacerbated and intensified the ancient comparison trap. We compare how many followers other people have and their projected happiness, success, and impact they are having in the world. Without knowing, through social media, we are often watching other people's edited, exaggerated, and glossy highlight reels.

A comparison is a pathway to unnecessary stress and anxiety. As Theodore Roosevelt insightfully said, "Comparison is the thief of joy." I know firsthand that comparison has been a thief of joy in my life.

There are two primary comparison pathways. Either way, comparing ourselves to others traps us in the *selfie-life*, whereby we become self-absorbed and self-critical.

Comparison can lead to feelings of superiority:

- *I'm smarter than you.*
- *I'm better than you.*
- *I'm stronger than you.*

Comparison can lead to feelings of inferiority:

- *I'm not smart enough.*
- *I'm not good enough.*
- *I'm not strong enough.*

Who have you compared yourself with in the past week? My counsel is simple:

1. Stay in your own lane
2. Run your own race at your own pace

THE SHAME PARASITE

The voice of shame in my experience has been lingering and lurking in my soul, resembling a parasite. A parasite is a foreign organism living on the inside or outside of another organism.

The host of shame is the vulnerable human soul. Shame feeds off and spreads through secrecy and hiddenness. The shame parasite speaks toxic words and simultaneously gags us into silent submission. As you can see, shame is deceptive and penetrates mercilessly deep into our soul—our identity, self-worth, and significance as a person. Through my lethal inner critic, I was slowly self-sabotaging and suffocating my life from an early age.

Amidst the traumatic incident on the Doonside soccer field, my inner resolve as a child was never to put myself in that situation ever again. My life mission would be to protect myself at all costs from experiencing any further public humiliation of perceived failure. Regrettably, I also deceived myself in believing failure is fatal and final.

SHAME TRIGGERS

We all experience defining moments of dysfunction throughout our lives. Such moments often falsely define who we are and, at times, who we are not; what we can do and what we cannot.

The ordeals of my first operation in the hospital and kicking the soccer ball out of play became two new triggers and adverse influences in my childhood.

Those two traumatic experiences have not only tortured my soul but sadly increased my vulnerability to mental health struggles later in life. Remember what I said in the prologue—*Shame was a pathway to my mental health struggle.*

What is your primary shame trigger?

Addiction
Adoption
Anxiety
Bankruptcy
Body image
Burnout
Chronic illness
Depression
Disability
Divorce
Failure
Gender
Humiliation

Moral failure
Nationality
Poverty
Rejection
Sexual abuse
Singleness
Trauma
Unemployment
Unmanageable debt
Other: _____

SHAME TRIGGERS (cont.)

How did that experience of shame make you feel?

_____

_____

If you're unsure, look at the table of unpleasant emotions. Circle all the emotions that describe your first experience of shame. Take a moment to feel that emotion. Where in your body do you feel the uncomfortable emotion of shame?

Likewise, for those struggling with fear, anxiety, or depression, circle all the accompanying emotions. Where in your body do you feel fear, anxiety, and depression? _____

_____

_____

Afraid	Angry	Anxious	Sad
fearful	furious	overwhelmed	unhappy
intimidated	frustrated	stressed	depressed
abandoned	agitated	humiliated	down
unaccepted	annoyed	trapped	devastated
weak	resentful	ashamed	unworthy
insecure	bitter	guilty	disappointed
vulnerable	irritable	embarrassed	regretful
insignificant	jealous	nervous	distressed
alienated	ticked off	suffocated	anguished
threatened	impatient	uncertain	sorrowful
restless	snappy	helpless	worthless

FURTHER THOUGHT AND CONTEMPLATION

Take a few minutes to be still and ponder these words from priest, author, and theologian Henri Nouwen:

> "A life without a quiet center, easily becomes destructive."

shame is an assessment

"The greatest weakness of all is the fear of appearing weak." —**Jacques-Bénigne Bossuet**

Throughout life, we are continually making assessments. For example, you walk past a close friend and smile, but they don't smile back. You might make an assessment: "They're angry with me."

Your child doesn't respond to a simple request. Once again, you might make an assessment: "They don't respect me."

Your boss doesn't respond to your important email. Similarly, you might make an assessment: "He (or she) doesn't value me."

An assessment transpires when we hastily and, at times, recklessly jump to a faulty conclusion. We instantly and subconsciously make a judgment or form an opinion about something or someone. We impulsively make assessments without considering our prejudices, biases, and blind spots.

It appears amusing now, but during my first year as a youth pastor of a church in Perth, I was bothered and unsettled by a highly-respected leader in our church. Every time I preached, within a few minutes he would habitually fold his arms and close his eyes. It was such a disheartening experience as a young and inexperienced preacher. I wondered, *Is he bored with my preaching? Is there nothing profound I can impart that may impact his life?*

Out of nowhere, after I preached one night, he asked if he could talk to me. My first thought was he was going to give me the negative feedback I expected. To my utter surprise, he explained his habit of closing his eyes when I preached.

Apparently, he found it helpful to close his eyes so he could better focus on what was being spoken. He also clarified he didn't want me to misunderstand him, and said he deeply appreciated my preaching.

In response, I pretended I never noticed his closed eyes or found his practice of concentration discouraging. I was relieved and embarrassed by my defective assessment.

Surely, you've done that at least once before?

Our common predicament in life is we fail to take the time to gather all the facts or even consider an alternate perspective. At times, and to our peril, we overestimate our ability to discern and genuinely understand the bigger picture or other possibilities to the scenario.

Shame is a paralysing assessment of oneself as a person. Shame is a voice that speaks and declares a faulty assessment in the disguise of truth, especially when we are hurting and emotionally vulnerable.

From my experience, I know firsthand how *a flawed assessment can lead to bitter resentment.*

WHERE'S DAD?

Many of you are likely familiar with the inspirational children's book series, *Where's Wally?* created by British illustrator Martin Handford. As the reader opens the pages of the book, they are dazzled by an impressive montage of people doing comical and crazy things.

The scene on each double page is complex and chaotic. The straightforward, yet frustrating, challenge of the book is to find the hidden Wally (or Waldo for people living in the USA or Canada), dressed in a dorky red and white striped outfit. *Where's Wally?*

The disturbing and unrelenting question during my childhood and teenage years was—*Where's Dad?*

Open the book of my troubled and fragmented life, and the challenge would be to find my dad attentively and affectionately engaged in my life:

Where was Dad when I played sports?

Where was Dad when I was struggling with homework?

Where was Dad when I was being bullied at school?

Where was Dad when I battled with rejection after my girl-friend dumped me?

Where was Dad when I toiled with deep personal issues, such as the confusion and awkwardness of puberty and my torment-ing shyness?

Where's Dad?

You have probably heard the statement "Your perception is your reality." My childhood perception was Dad's absence, exemplified by his lack of interaction, affection, and affirmation, was more of a reflection of who I was than who Dad was. Sadly, my faulty perception would soon become a damaging deception.

Why wasn't Dad more involved in my life?

Through the *vacuum of neglect,* I concluded it was my fault. Perhaps if I was a better son, a better student, or a better athlete, maybe then Dad would have been more engaged.

My reckless and faulty conclusion was Dad was absent because I was insignificant and worthless. For several years, I would experience a new manifestation of shame—the shame of perceived abandonment and neglect.

Through this flawed assessment, I once again allowed shame to speak and infuse my soul with additional venom. The problem with this is, I didn't have all the facts, and I couldn't access the whole story.

Could there be another reason why my dad was silent and disengaged as we walked home together after the soccer match?

Could there be another reason why Dad didn't help me practice my soccer skills after school?

The truth is, there was.

DEEP IMPACT

At the age of about ten, I had a typical conversation with my friends at school; as we bragged about what our dads (or the "old man") did for a living. The fact that we lived in the outer western suburbs of Sydney meant most of our dads were blue-collar, or working-class men.

My friends bragged for several minutes:

My dad's a carpenter.

My dad's a plumber.

My dad's a truck driver.

My dad works in a factory.

Then it came to my turn. With a sense of embarrassment, I confessed: "My dad doesn't work." Astonishment was abruptly followed by amusement. The fact was, Mum was a school teacher and the solitary breadwinner for about three years.

Why wasn't my dad working?

Dad was battling clinical depression. He was unemployed and possibly unemployable for a prolonged period of time. I'm talking about living with depression in the 1960s when there was no public awareness, understanding, or empathy. There were no celebrities or high profile athletes coming out from hiding and courageously sharing the journey of their mental health struggles.

Likewise, there were no helpful organisations like *Beyond Blue, Livin* or *RUOK*. All my dad and fellow sufferers with mental health issues could do was hide behind a veil of confusion, anger, humiliation, and shame.

My dad trained to be a local church pastor at the Churches of Christ Theological College in Melbourne. His first pastorate was in a small country church in northern Tasmania. Nevertheless, the experience was so stressful and traumatic, Dad left the ministry as a broken man.

Through God's enriching grace and supernatural healing, Dad courageously returned to ministry after an absence of about thirteen years. He was appointed as an associate pastor at Penrith Church of Christ, in NSW. After a couple of years and together with about twenty people, Dad pioneered a new church in Blaxland, in the majestic lower Blue Mountains.

There were other reasons why Dad was often disengaged. Like me, he suffered from the shame associated with his mental health struggle.

Now I understand that one of the reasons why Dad was often *emotionally discouraged* and *relationally disengaged*—he was endlessly enveloped in a dark cloud of depression, commonly known as the *Black Dog*. We were, in fact, intimately united as father and son through our pain—I just didn't realise it at the time.

As a child, I was somewhat protected by my naïvety, whereby I believed in the best of everything and everyone—including Dad. My world was once safe and secure. Despite this, something happened as I grew older. I suddenly became more aware of the frailty of life, including my own emotional dysfunction and unmet needs as a child during my formative years.

For decades, I have pondered the origin of my emotional turmoil. Am I merely the product of Dad's genes, like his height and long legs?

Personally, I see my battle with chronic anxiety more about possessing a *genetic vulnerability*, rather than a genetic predisposition.

At the end of the day, I am responsible for my mental health, and I can't blame Dad's rogue genes. Then again, there were times that I certainly did.

It is also possible that I have subconsciously seized and transferred Dad's shame onto myself. Consequently, his shame became my shame. His shame narrative became my shame narrative.

Living with a father battling depression and the allied collateral damage has unfortunately increased my vulnerability to the shame of debilitating mental health issues. And we are not alone.

DOWN UNDER

Here is a mental health snapshot of my nation:

* One in five Australians aged 16-85 experience mental illness each year.
* Forty-five per cent of Australians will be affected by mental illness in their lifetime.
* Aboriginal and Torres Strait Islander people are nearly three times more likely to suffer mental illness than other Australians and twice as likely to die by suicide.
* Every day, at least eight Australians die by suicide.
* Suicide is the leading cause of death for Australians between 15 and 44 years of age.

Further mental health facts and figures can be obtained from Beyond Blue, Black Dog Institute, Mental Health Council of Australia and The Australian Institute of Health and Welfare.

Something is fundamentally wrong within the soul of my nation. We have a popular saying in Australia: "She'll be right mate."

The fact is, she ain't right mate.

COURAGEOUS VULNERABILITY

Let's talk about vulnerability for a moment. To be vulnerable is to feel exposed, emotionally naked, and open to attack. If you feel vulnerable, you are not alone. To be vulnerable is to be human.

Give this some thought: from the moment of conception, life is uncertain, unsafe, unpredictable, and at times, unfair.

Below are some situations when I have felt vulnerable:

- My first day of school.

- Sitting in the dentist's waiting room.

- Falling in love.

- Starting Beachway Church (1994) and leaving Beachway Church (2017).

- Letting the church know that I'm seeing a therapist for chronic anxiety and panic attacks.

- Suffering gastro while preaching in India—one sneeze and I'm in big trouble.

- Writing this book.

When have you felt vulnerable? _____
_____
_____
_____

Examine the table below. With each vulnerable situation, there is a corresponding "What if..." question. After all, the heart of vulnerability is the fear of uncertainty.

Which situations can you relate to?

The Vulnerability Situation	The Vulnerability Question
Asking for help	What if I am judged?
Starting a new business	What if I fail?
Falling in love	What if I'm rejected?
Speaking in public for the first time	What if I make a fool of myself?
Your child is moody and withdrawn	What if he or she is on drugs?
Attempting to conceive	What if I can't get pregnant?
You're unemployed	What if I can't find work?
There's another interest rate rise	What if I can't pay the mortgage?
Forgiving a loved one after betrayal	What if I get hurt again?
Battling a chronic illness	What if I don't get better?
You're a single parent	What if I can't cope?
Ageing	What if I get dementia?
Other:	What if......................?

Where is God in our vulnerability? Is God distant and removed from our vulnerability? Does God merely tolerate our cries of vulnerability? Is God disappointed when we feel vulnerable?

1. **The birth of Jesus is a narrative of vulnerability**
   God experienced firsthand human vulnerability through the mystery of incarnation—*God became flesh.* At conception, the eternal Son of God was supernaturally reduced to a single fertilised egg within the womb of a Jewish virgin. The womb of a Jewish woman was a dangerous place to live under the violent reign of the Roman Empire during the first century.

2. **The ministry of Jesus is a narrative of vulnerability**
   After Jesus' baptism, He was driven into the wilderness by the Holy Spirit for an appointed time of testing. Jesus was alone and vulnerable before the dark forces of evil during His gruelling forty-day fast. Jesus was tempted to compromise His Sonship and mandate by miraculously turning stone into bread. The devil was smart enough not to tempt Jesus to perform this miracle on the first day of His fast. With astonishing courage, Jesus resisted the devil's persistent temptations. Yet, the wilderness experience was so distressing and exhausting, God sent angels to care for His Beloved Son [Matthew 4:11].

   We read in the book of Hebrews that Jesus was tempted in every way as we are, yet without sin [Hebrews 4:15]. Be assured, God has experienced and understands our vulnerability.

   During Jesus' ministry, He intentionally and compassionately connected with the marginalised and vulnerable of first-century society:

i. The sick: e.g., lepers, lame, mute, deaf and blind [Matthew 4:23-24].

ii. The spiritually and emotionally tormented: e.g., the Gerasene demoniac [Luke 8:26-37].

iii. The sexually fragmented: e.g., the Samaritan woman [John 4:4-42] and the woman caught in the act of adultery [John 8:1-11].

Discipleship, or following Jesus, is a radical journey of vulnerability. Jesus clearly warned His first disciples: "I am sending you out like sheep among wolves." [Matthew 10:16a]. Jesus didn't say, "I am sending you out like sheep among ducklings."

3. **The crucifixion of Jesus is a narrative of vulnerability**
From the cradle to the grave, Jesus experienced relentless vulnerability. While Jesus was dying on the cross, He didn't declare mantras He learnt from ancient self-help books such as:
Pain is weakness leaving My body.
This will make Me stronger.
I've got what it takes.
Stay calm.
No, in fact, many of Jesus' last words on the cross are expressions of unbearable pain and unimaginable vulnerability.

For example, Jesus cried out, "My God, My God, why have You forsaken Me?" [Matthew 27:46]

At this tender moment of torment, Jesus was calling out to His Father with the terrifying cry of abandonment, thus fulfilling an ancient prophecy found in Psalm

22. For the first time in eternity, the Beloved Son is forsaken by His Father because He is covered with the sin and shame of humanity. [See 2 Corinthians 5:21]

Jesus was utterly vulnerable on the cross—Jesus was covered with our sin, so we can be covered with His righteousness. Jesus was physically naked, so our spiritual and emotional nakedness can be compassionately covered.

Let me ask the question again—where is God in our vulnerability?

The reality is God is not *removed* from our vulnerability—God is *moved* by our vulnerability. The prophet Isaiah declared when we are distressed, God too is distressed (63:9).

Conversely, Jesus didn't come to earth to merely identify with our vulnerability. Jesus was sent by the Father to transform our vulnerability, so we too can overcome the vulnerabilities in this world.

What comes to mind when you hear the word vulnerability? How many of us view vulnerability as a sign of instability or weakness?

What we desperately need today is a paradigm shift concerning vulnerability. From my experience, navigating through the shame of chronic anxiety requires raw courage.

It takes courage to embrace our vulnerability and ask for help. It takes courage to feel our pain and confront our fear of being exposed and hurt—of addressing our "What if…" questions.

All the same, vulnerability needs a partner in the dance of our transformation. The perfect dance partner for vulnerability is faith. Faith is spelled R-I-S-K. The foundation of our faith is the unshakable reality that God is good and God is always with us.

In the popular and beloved 23rd Psalm, God invites us to courageously face our greatest vulnerability—death. David wrote, "Even when I walk through the dark valley of death, I will not be afraid, *for You are close beside me.*" (4, NLT, italics mine)

It is reassuring to know that Jesus is familiar with the dark terrain of pain, vulnerability, and death; yet He went through them victoriously. When we walk through the dark valleys of life, Jesus is wholly present with us. His presence is empowering, comforting, and reassuring.

Vulnerability is not a pathway to defeat. We can rise above our vulnerability because Jesus, our Great Shepherd, is with us and He will never forsake us.

Whatever dark valley you are in or is before you, you are not alone. Right now, hand over your fear and vulnerability to Jesus. Hold His nailed-pierced hand, and walk together through the dark valley of the unknown.

Complete this sentence: *Even though I walk through* ____

_____

_____ *I will not be afraid, for You are with me.*

What does the journey of vulnerability look like?

1. Accept our vulnerability.
This is the starting point of our journey with vulnerability. Don't fight, struggle, or resist the feeling of vulnerability. Accept the reality that to be vulnerable is to be human—you are not alone.

2. Embrace our vulnerability.

Only when we accept our vulnerability, can we then embrace our vulnerability. On Facebook, it is one thing to accept a friend request and another to embrace a new friend and do life with them. This is the time to intentionally lean into vulnerability and acknowledge that vulnerability is our friend and not our enemy.

3. Leverage our vulnerability.

This is the game changer on our journey. We now invite God to redeem and turnaround our vulnerability. This is the time when our pain can become our platform of service and transformational impact.

Today, I leverage my vulnerability by speaking and writing about my journey with shame and anxiety. The truth is, shame cannot coexist with transparency and vulnerability.

4. Celebrate our vulnerability.

As we learn to accept, embrace, and leverage our vulnerability, it's time to party. David experienced both quiet waters and dark valleys. In so doing, God prepared a table for David in the presence of his enemies [Psalm 23:5].

Imagine sitting at an enormous wooden dining table feasting with Jesus and countless other saints. Before you is an astonishing banquet, lined with delightful dishes and delicacies from around the world.

Meanwhile, your enemies are forced by God to watch the ecstatic celebration from a distance. Can you see the spirit of fear, anxiety, depression, shame, guilt, lust, greed, and the rest of the demonic realm, watching you celebrate your courageous vulnerability?

WEAK MADE STRONG

For as long as I can remember, I have always wanted to be strong. From an early age, I was mesmerised watching Tarzan on TV, starring former USA Olympic swimmer Johnny Weissmuller (1904-1984). Even though his speech was limited to "Me Tarzan, you Jane," in the innocent and impressionable eyes of a vulnerable boy, he had the perfect physique, and he was undeniably strong.

Added to my list of heroes of raw masculinity were:

- John Wayne (Actor)
- Neil Young (Musician)
- Graham Eadie (Rugby League)
- Simon Anderson (Surfing)
- Dennis Lillee (Cricket)
- Peter Brock (Motor Racing)
- John Newcombe (Tennis)

Collectively, they reinforced my faulty assessment of what it means to be a man who is strong and respected.

Weakness is greatly misunderstood in our society, and the consequences are massive. What makes matters worse, we live in a world that is, by and large, intolerant of weakness.

How often are we appalled in a sport when someone drops a catch, misses a goal or misses a putt?

One by one we have witnessed our sporting heroes, Hollywood celebrities, politicians, priests, and pastors publically and spectacularly implode. Once again, we are appalled, yet ironically entertained by their poor decision making, addictions, and worst of all, their public displays of weakness.

Of note, this book was not written during a fruitful and fulfilling season in my life. I wrote *SHAME OFF YOU* during a turbulent time when I felt emotionally weak and vulnerable. I just wonder, could there be an anointing in weakness?

We should be grateful that God doesn't expose our weaknesses to shame us, but instead, He exposes our weaknesses to transform us.

When God observes our weaknesses, He doesn't say, "Shame on you!" Rather He says, "Shame off you!"

WEAK IS THE NEW STRONG

Do any of these statements below sound familiar?

> *50 is the new 40.*
> *Orange is the new black.*
> *Risk is the new safe.*
> *Weird is the new normal.*
> *Small is the new big.*

These phrases reveal a new assessment or framework of perspective. With a new set of lenses, we can perceive a dramatic turnaround, whereby *something is the new something else.* Allow me to share another framework of thinking:

> *Weak is the new strong.*

As is evident by now, one of my consuming fears growing up was the fear of appearing weak. Yet, in God's Kingdom, there is a mysterious paradox—God's power works best in the context of human weakness. By God's grace, the weak are profoundly strong [2 Corinthians 12:9-10].

One implication is the place of our distress and brokenness is also the place of our anointing and enlargement.

It has taken me years to discover that we are at our Kingdom best through our vulnerabilities and weaknesses. Weak is the new strong.

ASSESSMENT ASSIGNMENT

Think of a time you made a faulty assessment about God, a family member, friend, work colleague, pastor, or yourself.

How did that assessment impact you? _____

_____

_____

_____

_____

How did that assessment make you feel? You may find it helpful to go back to the emotions table on page 30. _____

_____

_____

_____

_____

Where was the evidence that your assessment was true and accurate?_____

_____

_____

_____

_____

Could there be another possibility or perspective to consider? _____

_____

_____

_____

_____

FURTHER THOUGHT AND CONTEMPLATION

Take a few minutes to be still and ponder these words from author and speaker Graham Cooke:

> "The passion of God that kills our strength
> now nurtures our weakness into a place of
> joyful vulnerability."

shame is a narrative

"So often, when facing our own giants, we
forget what we ought to remember and we
remember what we ought to forget."
—Charles Swindoll

Shame is a misleading, perverted, and prejudiced author,
daily scripting our life narrative. Like all books, our life narrative contains scenarios, beliefs, paragraphs, chapters, settings, themes, plots, and fascinating places and characters.
Shame skillfully and deceitfully writes a script that appears
real and truthful but is more often fabricated and malicious.

Shame is a narrative, or more precisely, a "self-narrative."
A self-narrative is a story you tell yourself about yourself.

Essentially, the theme of our self-narrative is always the
same. Sure, the details of the time, place, people, and circumstances may differ. For many people like myself, the fundamental theme or premise of our self-narrative is shame. Unless we're on our guard, our self-narrative can easily evolve
unforgivingly, into a "shame narrative."

The shame narrative is relentlessly repeating and reinforcing a contrived and harmful tale, such as:

You're incompetent.
You're inadequate.
You're inferior.

You're incapacitated.
You're disqualified.
You're insignificant.
You're invalid.

What is the story you tell yourself about yourself?

Like my shame narrative about the hospital episode and soccer match, write down a couple of defining moments that have shaped the way you view yourself and the world. _____

_____
_____
_____
_____
_____
_____
_____
_____
_____
_____

What would be the title of your self-narrative? _____

_____
_____
_____
_____
_____
_____
_____
_____
_____
_____

THE SHAME NARRATIVE

The Bible is a narrative about shame. If you were to read the Bible with a different set of lenses, you would notice there is a tragic narration of our unrelenting journey with brokenness provoked by shame.

Here are a few ancient examples:

- Adam and Eve: the shame of nakedness [Genesis 3:10].

- Abraham and Sarah: the shame of barrenness [Genesis 16:1 ff].

- Joseph: the shame of false accusations and imprisonment [Genesis 39:1-23].

- Gideon: the shame of weakness and hiding [Judges 6:11-16].

- Naomi: the shame of widowhood [Ruth 1:6-13, 19-22].

- Mephibosheth: the shame of a disability [2 Samuel 9:1-13].

- David: the shame of adultery [2 Samuel 11:1ff].

- Tamar: the shame of rape and incest [2 Samuel 13:1-22].

- Israel: the shame of slavery [through the ferocious tyranny of the Egyptian, Babylonian and Roman Empires].

- The haemorrhaging woman: the shame of impurity and exploitation [Mark 5:24-34].

- Bartimaeus: the shame of blindness, poverty, and begging [Mark 10:46-52].

- The Canaanite woman: the shame of being a Gentile or a non-Jewish "outsider" [Matthew 15:21-28].

- The ten lepers: the shame of leprosy and spiritual uncleanness [Luke 17:11-19].

- Zacchaeus: the shame of being a tax collector and a national traitor [Luke 19:1-10].

- Peter: the shame of denial [Matthew 26:69-75].

- Judas: the shame of betrayal [Matthew 27:1-10].

- Paul: the shame of sin [Romans 7:14-25].

WHERE ARE YOU?

What is the origin of the universal shame narrative? We read in the book of Genesis, the ancient and sacred creation narrative, that the first humans were naked and yet they felt no shame:

"The two of them, the Man and his Wife, were naked, *but they felt no shame.*" [Genesis 2:25, MSG, italics mine]

Adam and Eve were naked, innocent, and felt no shame. Neither of them was afraid of being exposed, exploited, or endangered. They were never intimidated, angry, jealous, judgmental, or suspicious of each other.

There was not a moment when they were self-conscious, self-absorbed, or self-righteous. For instance, Eve never asked Adam, "Are my thighs getting bigger?" Equally,

Adam was not alarmed and confused about what the "right answer" would be.

Yet, as the narrative unfolds, it appears that out of nowhere everything goes horribly wrong. Adam and Eve have done the unthinkable—they have rebelled and sinned against God. Could everything be eternally lost for humanity?

God graciously approaches the couple during the "cool of the day" [Genesis 3:8]. Once more, they have an opportunity to encounter a fresh manifestation of God's glorious and majestic presence.

We can only imagine there was usually anticipation and delight of this unhindered experience, of God walking in the garden during the cool of the day.

Tragically, God the Father asked the heartbreaking question, "Where are you?" [Genesis 3:9] The three words "Where are you?" is more of a statement than a question. After all, God knows everything about everything; God knows exactly where they are hiding and why they are hiding.

The first humans had been abruptly and painfully exposed. The moment they sinned against God, their eyes were immediately opened, and they knew they were naked. Instinctively, they covered up their sin and shame of nakedness on their terms, and using their methods—they made a temporary covering by sewing "fig leaves" together [Genesis 3:7].

For the first time in history, humans were consumed with fear as they hid from God's presence. The benevolent presence of God was now an imminent threat, not a magnificent delight.

This is the *catastrophic birth of shame.*

HIDE AND FREAK

Hide-and-seek is a popular game played by children of all ages throughout the world. There are variations to the rules, but basically, you require a designated seeker and a group of hiders.

The seeker closes their eyes and counts out loud (e.g. to fifty) while the other players hide. The seeker then opens their eyes and says something like, "Ready or not, here I come!"

The mission of the seeker is to find all the hiders. The first one found is usually the next seeker, and the last is the winner of the round.

The beauty of this game is it doesn't cost money, and it's an opportunity to be creative by finding an obscure place to hide.

When God asked the question, "Where are you?" it wasn't the first game of hide-and-seek. For people like myself living with shame—hiding is not a game, and it is far from fun.

Withdrawing and hiding is painful, yet a matter of safety and survival. The thought of being found and exposed is alarming and terrifying.

Recall an experience which made you want to run and hide.

SHAME COVERINGS

God continues to ask humanity the same disturbing questions as our ancient ancestors: "Where are you?" And, "Why are you hiding?"

Covering our spiritual and emotional nakedness is a universal defence against being exposed. Like Adam and Eve, we continue to hide our shame on our terms and using our methods. We have advanced from covering our shame with fig leaves to a shrewder and more subtle selection of coverings.

Let's take a moment to investigate the popular fashion styles of our shame coverings. Together, they temporarily relieve stress, compensate what we have lost, distract us from reality, and numb our troubled soul.

1. **Busyness**
   Ask many people today how they're doing, and their first response will likely be "I'm busy!" What's that all about? Has busyness become the badge of honour and self-worth in the 21st Century? We need to pause and consider—"Busy doing what?" and more significantly, "Busy *being* what?"

   Why are we so preoccupied with busyness? Could the underlying message of "I'm busy." be "I'm important?" When we're continually busy, we fail to be still and create a sacred space for God to reveal His unfailing love amidst our distressing pain.

2. **Entertainment**
   As a child growing up in the 1960s, my family went to the cinema infrequently because of financial hardship. The family outing began with the thrill of catching the train, affectionately known as the *Red Rattler*, from Doonside to Toongabbie or Parramatta. Another treat was eating Choc Top ice creams or popcorn while watching cinema classics such as *The Sound of Music* and *Chitty Chitty Bang Bang*.

Occasionally, we could stay up late on Friday night (8:30PM) and watch Bill Collins *Golden Years of Holly-wood* on TV.

Today is entirely different. With cable TV, Foxtel and Netflix, we can spend numerous hours every day being excessively entertained, thereby avoiding the demands and challenges of modern living.

3. Addictions

Like entertainment, there has never been a time in history when we have been more medicated and addicted. Take your pick of addictions from alcohol, drugs (including sleeping medication), sugar, pornography, gambling, work, social media, and video games.

Today, we even have amusing addiction statements such as:

- *Adrenalin rush.*
- *Caffeine fix.*
- *Sugar hit.*
- *Comfort eating.*
- *Retail therapy.*

These statements subtly soften the gravity and impact of our crippling addictions.

4. Perfectionism

I'm a walking contradiction at times. In some areas of my life I am disciplined and a restless perfectionist. Yet, in other areas, I'm a chronic and troubled procrastinator.

Some may argue that perfectionism is a form of procrastination. In any case, a perfectionist is desperately seeking order and control. There was a time, when I was a young adult, when my wardrobe was so orderly, that the colour of my shirts matched the colour of the coat hanger. Yes, I desperately needed therapy.

If I was unable to manage stress, I would go straight to the pantry—not to eat, but to reorganise the items in categories (herbs, spices, cereal, condiments, etc.) and in descending order of size.

5. Chronic shyness

My innate shyness came to the surface during my teenage years, especially when it involved girlfriends. First, there was the dread of asking a girl out on a date. Then, as the relationship surprisingly progressed, taking the initiative to hold her hand was embarrassingly stressful.

What didn't help my flight was some people in the youth group were publically highlighting my shyness, pressuring on me to "man up." From my experience, shyness was more than being an introvert—shyness was a form of self-protection and a garment to cover my shame.

6. Religion

Tragically, religion can be another garment of temporary and futile covering. Religion without grace will always be divisive. People with a "religious spirit" inevitably define and determine who is in their tribe and who is out of their tribe. Likewise, religion can seduce people into an erroneous perception that they are right and everyone outside their tribe is wrong.

Jesus didn't come to earth to start another religion. Jesus came to activate a radical love revolution characterised by a spirit of inclusiveness, forgiveness, and reckless mercy.

7. **Other**

There are numerous other shame coverings.
How many can you identify?
What is your preferred shame covering? Why? _____

_____

_____

_____

THE PADDLE OF SHAME

Here is another episode of my shame narrative. One of my first experiences of intense and overwhelming panic was while surfing with a close friend at Scarborough Beach, located 13km northwest of Perth. Surfing at Scarborough Beach (affectionately known as *Scarbs*) can at times be a frustrating experience, with inconsistent swell and persistent onshore winds.

Conversely, there are those rare days when *Scarbs* is "going off," and I recall one such day. *Scarbs* is known for its shallow sandbanks and can handle a solid 3-meter swell. It was one of those moments many an amateur surfer dreads. A monster set was approaching my way, and the decision was simple, but it had to be resolute.

I thought to myself, *Do I wait for the wave to come to me and dive under the impact zone or do I attempt to paddle over it?* In a second, I chose the latter. There can be no room for hesitation. As a surfer in this situation, you must be 100 per cent committed, and I was.

With all the strength remaining after a couple of hours surfing, I paddled frantically towards the intimidating wall of the Indian Ocean.

The last couple of strokes are the most crucial, and as I penetrated the thick lip of the giant wave one last time, I felt relief, and I thought to myself, *I've made it.*

It can only be described as a horrifying feeling when the thick, impenetrable lip of the wave unexpectedly pitches you mercilessly backwards. Surfers call this dreaded encounter "going over the falls." You hit the water beneath so powerfully and violently, your breath is literally taken away, and everything goes terrifyingly dark and chaotic.

Despite years of experience in similar situations, I made a detrimental mistake—I panicked. There is nothing worse than being held under turbulent water and tossed around fiercely like you're inside a washing machine during the spin cycle. To make matters worse, I made another error by closing my eyes while under water. That only intensified my sense of disorientation and panic.

After several seconds of being held under, I began to see stars and thought this was it—*I'm going to drown!* When I finally made it to the surface, I took a deep breath, with the unsettling sense of panic increasing in my body, I paddled desperately back to shore. That terrifying encounter with the ocean was my *paddle of shame.*

Apart from my erratic breathing and the uncomfortable sensation of adrenaline pulsating through my weary body, my thinking over the following minutes became perilously irrational and catastrophic:

I nearly drowned.
I never want to be in that situation again.
I don't have what it takes to surf big waves.
I'm not a strong surfer.
My mind is weak... hang on. I am weak.

BREATHE

The average person can survive without food for forty days, five days without water and up to eleven days without sleep—apparently. On the contrary, when it comes to precious oxygen, the average person without extensive "breath hold" training can only survive about four minutes.

Breathing is an essential part of life. Breathing is life. Breathing is fuel. For most of us, breathing is something we do subconsciously, and it is not a cause for distress. After all, breathing is natural, automatic, and involuntary; we rarely need to think about it.

Some of the exceptions would be people who suffer from respiratory conditions such as asthma, pneumonia, and emphysema. For them, breathing is a serious issue and battle in their life.

Elite athletes also understand the importance of effective breathing to remain calm, composed, and focused. Through sports like extreme surfing in iconic surf breaks such as Mavericks (northern California) and Teahupoo (Tahiti), a surfer discovers in dangerous situations just how far one breath hold can take them. When it's all said, and done, breathing in extreme conditions is all about extensive and rigorous stress management.

Nevertheless, there is another group of people who are always aware of the importance and anguish of breathing. Together, we hide behind a veil of shame—the debilitating and humiliating condition commonly known as *panic attacks*.

PANIC STATIONS

Although panic attacks are not life-threatening, from personal experience, I can confirm they are a terrifying and horrendous experience. Panic attacks occur unexpectedly, swiftly, and abruptly.

Many people find their first panic attack is their worst, just because they don't know what is happening to them. This is only compounded if your first panic attack strikes mercilessly while you're in a public place.

Everyone is different, but for most people experiencing a panic attack report they have trouble breathing and suffer dizziness, trembling, sweating, choking, nausea, and a rapid heartbeat. Not surprisingly, a panic attack can easily be mistaken for a heart attack.

Panic attacks can happen anywhere and at any time. I have experienced the terror of panic attacks in the following places:

- Restaurants
- Movie theatres
- Shopping centres
- Sitting in the car at traffic lights
- During a conference
- Out in the surf
- Flying
- While asleep

Each attack is unpredictable and unbearable. If that's not enough, now add the tormenting shame of having a panic attack in a public place.

In Australia, up to 40 per cent of the population will experience a panic attack at some stage in their life. [www. healthdirect.gov.au]

Imagine continuously living on high alert. After the first panic attack, you now become anxious about when and where the next panic attack may occur. Will it be worse than the first one? In turn, you panic about panic. That's right—*panic begets panic.*

Incidentally, it's not over when the panic attack subsides. You then feel utterly humiliated and exhausted by the experience. It can sometimes take hours before you feel any sense of calm, focus, and normality.

Think for a moment of the term *panic attack.* I can appreciate that if you were attacked by a ferocious bear, there's a good reason to be infused with adrenaline, so your whole physiology is ready to either:

1. Fight the bear.
2. Freeze before the bear.
3. Flight or flee from the bear.

Whether you choose to fight, freeze or flee the bear, you would be rightly labelled as courageous. Even so, in my world, I am not being attacked by a wild bear. I am merely being attacked by an irrational thought, and an invisible sensation called "panic."

People around you cannot see or feel your panic. All they can do is say well-meaning statements like:

Don't panic.
It's all in your head.
Man up.

Snap out of it.
Push through.
Just relax.
Pray harder.
Have more faith.
What you need to do is …

MEET AMY

What is happening below the surface of a panic attack?

It's time for you to meet Amy. Fear and anxiety are first provoked in the *amygdala,* pronounced *uh-mig-duh-luh.* The amygdala is a double almond-shaped structure located in the temporal lobes of our brain.

American author and entrepreneur Seth Godin refers to our amygdala as the "lizard brain." It is the primal part of our brain that is hardwired for our protection and survival, thereby limiting our vulnerability.

I find it helpful to think of my amygdala as Amy—the first three letters of the word *amy*-gdala. Yes, there are two women in my life—my darling wife Karen and Amy, my intimate danger detector.

Amy constantly and thoroughly scans my outside world for potential threats. Unfortunately, Amy cannot always differentiate between a real threat and a perceived threat. For example, Amy cannot tell the difference between the threat of facing a bear, versus the threat of speaking in public for the first time. From Amy's primal perspective, both events are detected as hazardous.

Throughout my life, Amy has overreacted and unintentionally misled me. Amy means well; after all, she is looking out for me. Amy desperately wants me to be safe and survive. Yet, if you're not careful, in my experience, Amy can dominate your brain and derail your life.

To be fair, I can't blame Amy for continually overreacting and releasing uncomfortable amounts of stress hormones such as *adrenaline, norepinephrine, and cortisol* throughout my body. After all, I am the one who has supplied Amy with incorrect and unreliable data over the decades. Amy is just doing her primal job.

With that in mind, let's now uncover the profound relationship between Amy (our amygdala) and panic attacks. Panic attacks can be described as an internal terror experienced throughout our whole being.

When Amy detects a threat, miraculously within milliseconds our anxious and fearful thoughts activate our *fight-freeze-flight* stress response, releasing an overwhelming and uncomfortable cascade of stress hormones. Our heart rate, blood pressure, and breathing increases instantly and dramatically, preparing us to respond to the challenge of the potential threat.

Over the years, I have had candid discussions with Amy. For example, I have demanded evidence from Amy that the threat is imminent and genuinely life-threatening. Amy has had to discover that there are times in life when the unfamiliar, leaving my comfort zone, and taking on risks are good for me.

My intention is not to ignore Amy, but to calm her down. Amy needs constant reassurance that there is more to life than safety and survival.

One of my "wellbeing ploys" is to courageously and repetitiously do something which I am afraid of. As I do, remarkably new neural pathways are forged throughout my pliable brain, and over time Amy is slowly learning to chill out.

THE BREATH OF LIFE

Through deep breathing, we can remarkably switch or reset our body's nervous system from a sympathetic state (arousal of *fight-freeze-flight*) to a more desirable parasympathetic state *(rest-digest-heal)*—consequently, the way we breathe impacts how we feel and how we perform.

The following breathing exercises can help prevent, or at least diminish the impact of a panic attack. More than that, regular deep breathing can help you prepare for an exam, a presentation or a significant sporting event.

I regularly use breathing exercises before I preach, have an awkward conversation, engage in a pastoral crisis, work out at the gym, and before I go to sleep.

BREATHING 101

3:3:3

This is the first breathing exercise I learnt from my therapist. The 3:3:3 method is ideal if you have never performed a breathing exercise before.

Inhale to the count of **3**
Hold your breath to the count of **3**
Exhale to the count of **3**

3:4:5

Inhale to the count of **3**
Hold your breath to the count of **4**
Exhale to the count of **5**

4:7:8

Inhale to the count of **4**
Hold your breath to the count of **7**
Exhale to the count of **8**

5:5:5:5

This is also known as "box breathing." I first heard about box breathing from former Navy SEAL Mark Divine's superb book, *The Way of the Seal*.

Inhale to the count of **5**
Hold your breath to the count of **5**
Exhale to the count of **5**
Hold your breath to the count of **5**

BREATHING TIPS

1. Breathe through your nose.
Avoid breathing in through your mouth. This technique slows down and controls the amount of oxygen you inhale, hence preventing the unpleasant experience of hyperventilating.

2. Breathe through your belly.
Concentrate on your belly or diaphragm as you breathe, rather than your chest. You may find it helpful to place your hands on your belly and feel the gentle movement of slow rhythmic breathing.

3. Visualise a peaceful scene while breathing.
While breathing deeply and slowly, think attentively about a scene that is beautiful and tranquil. It may be a mountain range, river, lake, sunset, or an eagle in flight.

4. Play peaceful music while breathing.
Create a playlist of your favourite relaxation music.

5. Repeat life-giving phrases while breathing.
The words we speak over our lives can impact our physiology either positively or negatively. Words have the power to release life or death [Proverbs 18:21].

BREATHING TIPS (cont.)

The following are examples of life-giving words or *mantras* that you can quietly recite while breathing deeply:

God is my strength.
Fear not; God is with me.
This will make me stronger.
Be still and know God.
I've got this.
I am loved.
God is on the throne.
Ruthless trust.
Live loved.
He restores my soul.
Peace, be still.
Slow down.
Calm.
Other: _____

BREATHING NINJA

Do you want to become a breathing ninja?

1. Experiment with the various breathing exercises over a few weeks and discover which one works best for you.

2. Make deep breathing an integral part of your daily routine—perform your favourite breathing exercise for about five minutes in the morning and five minutes in the evening.

Let me introduce to you a helpful breathing proverb: *Confidence comes from competence.*

Confidence in the health benefits of belly breathing is an overflow of competence. And the only way to become competent in belly breathing is through daily practice over a minimum of two months.

The more you practice belly breathing, the more you master your breath and have unshakable confidence in your ability to dramatically reduce the impact of panic at any time, at any place, and in any situation.

Stop reading this book for a moment and try the 3:3:3 breathing exercise for three minutes.

Breathe slowly through your nose and activate your belly. Visualise a peaceful scene and simply... *breathe.*

There's no pressure to make anything happen, *just be and breathe.*

Remain calm and focus on your breath.

Breathe in life and breathe out tension.

Breathe in the Spirit of God and breathe out the spirit of despair.

Breathe...

FURTHER THOUGHT AND CONTEMPLATION

Shame can only be healed once it has been exposed. God continues to reveal our shame to heal our shame.

Spend a few minutes alone and imagine living without shame. What would a shame-free life look like and feel like?

shame is a weight

"Anxiety weighs down the heart…"
—Proverbs 12:25

For those of us who suffer and struggle with our emotional health, we are also overwhelmed and overburdened with shame. Shame is an agonising and, at times, an unbearable weight. Shame is burdensome and relentlessly heavy. Shame is the extra and unnecessary baggage we carry throughout life, and it's utterly exhausting.

In the previous chapter, I shared a story about a severe wipeout while surfing at Scarborough Beach. Unfortunately, that was not an isolated incident. There have been further episodes in my "shame narrative" regarding my struggle to breathe and manage stress. Shame is compounding and has continuously weighed me down and crushed my spirit.

THE THAI EXPRESS

In January 2007, we were relaxing in Singapore while on family holidays. Together we were enjoying swimming at the hotel pool, working out at the gym, shopping, and eating out.

One evening we went to the *Thai Express* for dinner, a local restaurant known for its authentic and affordable Asian dishes. When the waiter took our order, she mentioned the dish I ordered was exceptionally spicy.

I grew up on lamb chops, mashed potatoes, carrots, and peas. My only experience of spice was Heinz Tomato Sauce. Over the past several years, I have experimented and increased my appreciation and tolerance for chilli. So, I thought to myself, "Bring it on."

After a few mouthfuls of eating my meal, I was both overcome by the exquisite Asian flavours and the intensifying impact of the chilli that was beyond what I had experienced before.

It happened so quickly and abruptly. My recollection is it felt like some chilli was lodged inside my throat and my oesophagus instantly closed. I was immediately agitated because I couldn't breathe in and I couldn't breathe out. Once again, like my wipeout at Scarborough Beach, I panicked.

The sight and sound of me gasping intensely for oxygen understandably caused my children, Emily and Jake, to scream hysterically. The people around me in the restaurant were naturally alarmed, and the manager frantically came to our aid, asking Karen if I need an ambulance. Hearing the word "ambulance" exasperated the situation. My friend Amy was on high alert and gravely concerned for my welfare.

The incident was surreal and horrifying. Karen had only recently shared with me that Emily had been experiencing reoccurring nightmares in which I tragically died. As a good mother, Karen reassured Emily that wouldn't happen—certainly not while I'm in my forties.

As I was frantically trying to breathe, I remember thinking I am going to die in front of Emily and her faith in God will be shattered. Just like the surfing incident at Scarborough Beach, I couldn't breathe, and I thought I was going to die. And yes, my thinking was once again catastrophic.

Over several minutes my breathing improved, we finished our meal, paid the bill and went back to our hotel room. Before the lights went out, I did my best to reassure Emily—who was still upset—that everything was going to be okay and she had no reason to be anxious.

Who was I kidding? Anxious! That's the emotion that began to dominate and debilitate my private world. It felt like my life was abruptly *derailed* while eating at the *Thai Express.*

CHOKER

After a restless night of sleep, as I continually replayed the alarming scenario at the *Thai Express,* we went downstairs for breakfast. I filled my plate from the buffet with eggs, bacon, pancakes, and a variety of tropical fruit.

As I took my first mouthful of eggs and bacon, I was overcome with a bizarre feeling I had never experienced before. As I was *chewing,* I was afraid to swallow. My heart was racing, and I was preoccupied with fearful thoughts. *What if I choke again? What if I have another episode like last night?*

The fear of choking plagued me for several months. Combined with the feeling of agitation, dizziness, rapid breathing, and an erratic heartbeat, it was caused by unbearable stress hormones released throughout my body.

What's happening to me?
What's wrong with me?
Am I losing the plot?

I can no longer execute two natural and necessary life skills that even a two-year-old can perform with ease—*I can't breathe and I can't swallow.*

In the world of sports, the term "choker" is an ugly and humiliating word. It's a word assigned to a person who is unable to perform with excellence under pressure, thereby missing an easy putt (golf), basket (basketball), volley (tennis) or goal (football).

Ironically, the word "anxious" stems from the Latin word "angere," which means "to press tight" or "choke." [Online Etymology Dictionary, https://www.etymonline.com]

For decades, I felt like a choker in life. The voice and weight of shame continued to harass and strangle me:

You're weak!
You're hopeless!
You're a choker!
SHAME ON YOU!

WEIGHT WATCHERS

Spend time reflecting on the ways shame has recently weighed you down. How has the weight of shame impacted your:

Faith _____
_____
_____

Mental health _____
_____
_____

Sleep _____
_____
_____

Relationships _____
_____
_____

Work or study _____
_____
_____

Confidence _____
_____
_____

Joy _____
_____
_____

THE BIGGEST LOSER CHALLENGE

Popular reality TV shows like *Australia's Biggest Loser* have entertained, informed, and inspired us since 2006. The progressive transformation of the contestants' minds, souls, and bodies have been extraordinary.

One of the highlights occurs near the end of the program. The remaining few contestants go on a long and gruelling hike, carrying the weight they have lost during the contest. For most of the contestants, this exercise is a brutal and unforgettable reminder of the impact that their excessive weight has had on their lives.

Imagine how freeing and transforming life would be to have such a significant weight removed.

Ready for something different?*

Plan and go on a 1km walk, carrying an item in a backpack that is heavy but within appropriate limits for your body weight and fitness level.

As you walk, feel and visualise the weight of shame, and reflect on how shame has relentlessly burdened your life.

Now, like the contestants of *Australia's Biggest Loser,* remove your backpack and shout with conviction—"SHAME OFF ME!"

---

* **Warning:** Do not attempt this exercise if you have a heart condition or high blood pressure.

SHAME SENSES

1. If I could see shame, it would look like: _____

_____

_____

_____

_____

2. If I could hear shame, it would sound like: _____

_____

_____

_____

_____

3. If I could taste shame, it would taste like: _____

_____

_____

_____

_____

4. If I could smell shame, it would smell like: _____

_____

_____

_____

_____

5. If I could touch shame, it would feel like: _____

_____

_____

_____

_____

[Adapted from Dr. Brené Brown, *I thought it was just me (but it isn't)*, 2007]

FURTHER THOUGHT AND CONTEMPLATION

Take a few minutes to be still and ponder these words from author and preacher Max Lucado:

> "If pride is what goes before a fall, then shame is what keeps you from getting up after one."

PERSONAL NOTES

shame is a posture

"To be alive is to be broken."
—Brennan Manning

How many of us remember being corrected by a parent, teacher, personal trainer, or physiotherapist, because of our poor posture?

Stop slouching.
Sit up straight.
Shoulders back.
Chin up.
Use your knees when lifting.

Good posture is essential, whether you're a weightlifter, ballet dancer, soldier, or sitting all day in an office. Sound posture can reduce back and neck pain; while improving breathing, focus, and mood.

Shame is a posture. Shame dictates the way we stand, sit, and walk. Shame endeavours to belittle and compel us to disappear, hide, or to at least remain unnoticed.

Not surprisingly, the word shame begins with the letters "sh." Shame is daily whispering these toxic declarations into our soul:

Shhh… you don't want to stand out in the crowd.

Shhh… you don't want to make a fool of yourself.
Shhh… you don't want to be unmasked.
Shhh… what will people think?
Sound familiar?

Shame can subconsciously trigger us to become overly self-conscious and self-protective. While speaking to people, we inadvertently fold our arms, cross our legs, cover our mouths, and avoid eye contact.

AWKWARD MOMENT

The excruciating weight of shame has undoubtedly impacted my posture. As a teenager, there was nothing worse than having a dramatic growth spurt, accompanied by paralysing shyness. That was me. Yes, I was one of those gangly and awkward teenagers. The last thing I wanted to do as a self-conscious teenager was stand out in the crowd and be exposed as weak.

In my third year of theological college, I was a youth pastor of a thriving church near Cronulla, south of Sydney. One Sunday after I preached, one of the young people amusingly impersonated my preaching posture. Her head was pointed down to the ground, and her shoulders and back were hunched over like Victor Hugo's fictitious character—the hunchback bell-ringer of the Notre Dame Cathedral.

She possibly exaggerated my posture to make a point. Even so, several other young people joined in and laughed. I know it was innocent fun, and I covered my humiliation by laughing with them—at my own expense of course.

There is no doubt that years of shyness, fear, anxiety, and shame were taking its toll. My posture gradually changed, reflecting my constant state of feeling inferior, overwhelmed, burdened, and ashamed. I thought I had effectively covered my shame, but once again my shame was publically exposed and I was in the spotlight for all the wrong reasons.

CURVEBALL

There was no doubt in my mind that 2007 was shaping to be one of the most momentous years in ministry. We were a church of 200-plus people and growing beyond our wildest dreams. There was a tangible presence of God in our Sunday services; lives were being changed for eternity, and we had recently raised $100,000 for community development locally and abroad.

Then there was *The Beach House.* Imagine, if you can, 1,500 square metres of space filled with a three-level play frame, bouncy castles, arcade games, climbing wall, car track, themed party rooms, and a stylish café. In a typical week, over 800 people from all over Perth would walk through our doors.

What also gave us confidence was the timely appointment of a young, dynamic and high-capacity couple as our associate pastors. At last, I was released to focus on preaching, pastoral care, contemplation, and raising new leaders. We were brilliantly poised for considerable growth and impact in our city and beyond.

In February, my friend and mentor from Sydney arrived to spend a weekend with our church. I can't recall a year where my expectations for growth were at an all-time high. I was even uncharacteristically confident in what was before us. "Time to put on our seatbelts," I reasoned, "because we're going to be in for a ride of our lives."

It was Friday evening, and I booked a local Italian restaurant for our mentor to meet with Karen, me, and our new associate pastors. Abruptly, within a few minutes of our lively conversation and even before we were served, I knew something was horribly wrong. The sensation was overwhelming and terrifying. It was the *Thai Express* revisited… but intensified.

My heart was pounding, my chest was tight, and once again I was having trouble breathing. Even before eating anything, I had an overpowering fear of choking. *This can't be happening*, I thought to myself. *Not now*.

Without thinking of how foolish this might appear and what people would think, I abruptly left the restaurant, ran outside and sat despairingly in my car. Unbeknown to me at the time, but I had a severe panic attack. Karen was left to reassure our newly appointed associate pastors that everything is okay.

My mentor joined me in my car. I was sobbing and shaking uncontrollably. In my mind, I resolved that I was having a nervous breakdown and would shortly be admitted to a psychiatric ward.

My thinking was once again irrational and catastrophic. I recklessly convinced myself that I have no choice but to resign from ministry immediately. At the same time, my body was bursting with unbearable levels of the stress hormones.

Yes, Amy was working strenuously.

What was wrong with me?

Was I going crazy?

My soul was painfully hemorrhaging. Shame had resurfaced once again in my life. But more than resurfaced, *shame had now become disturbingly personified*.

Shame was no longer an uncomfortable emotion, a voice, weight, or condition that I was combatting.

Shame was now a person.

Shame was Rob Mason.

WHY I SAW A THERAPIST

My first appointment with a therapist was on Monday morning, only two days after my terrifying and humiliating episode in the Italian Restaurant. The residue of my severe panic attack remained in my body.

As I was driving to Cottesloe, there was a severe thunderstorm. Growing up in Sydney, I loved the thunderstorms accompanying the "southerly buster" that often followed a hot and humid summer day.

On the contrary, during this susceptible stage of my life, as I was learning to navigate through chronic anxiety, loud noises and bright lights only heightened my level of panic. My body was continually on high alert and overacting. It was emotionally exhausting.

When I arrived in the therapist's office, still recovering from driving during a thunderstorm and after a brief, yet polite introduction, I explained my debilitating dilemma. I desperately wanted to go on medication and for her to fix my problem, and I thought now would be a good time for that to happen.

This recurring issue of panic and impaired breathing convinced me I had once and for all been exposed. My panic attack was a wakeup call and a defining moment of weakness, whereby I believed my faults and flaws were publically exposed. I instinctively knew that life would no longer be business as usual.

For people like me who have suffered from unmanageable anxiety and panic, we become acutely in tune with our physiology. We can get to a point when we sense even the slightest change to the rhythm of our heart and breathing. We also know when there has been the slightest surge of adrenaline, and we immediately feel agitated and restless.

The problem is we can come to the faulty conclusion that anxiety is purely physiological and all we need to recover and get on with life is medication. How wrong I was.

THINKING FOR A CHANGE

I had no idea that my journey of recovery firstly required dozens of hours of therapy. The issue wasn't merely changing the symptoms of anxiety, but changing the way I think and respond to stress.

A close friend in our church who is a mental health nurse, recommended I meet a colleague of hers who is a Cognitive Behavioural Therapist (CBT). *A CB what?* I deliberated.

Cognitive Behavioural Therapy is a psychological treatment for people like me struggling with chronic anxiety and panic attacks. A CBT therapist will assist you to identify unhealthy thoughts and beliefs and problematic behaviours that trigger anxiety.

Through CBT, you will learn new skills such as how to change your thinking, relaxation, and breathing techniques.
[Psychological treatments for Anxiety, www.beyondblue.org.au]

Over the past several years, I have learnt the hard way that anxiety is shaped primarily by my defective thinking and not my difficult circumstances.

In my fragile mind, I regularly and subconsciously interpreted situations for the worst and made hasty assumptions.

Not surprisingly, my anxious thoughts made me anxious, and poor Amy was continually and unnecessarily on high alert.

For the first time in my life, I was challenged to think about my thinking. Through the slow and humbling journey of therapy, I realised so much of my everyday thinking was negative, irrational, exaggerated, and catastrophic.

The problem with anxious thinking is that what we focus on, we strengthen. As we focus on anxious thoughts, we strengthen and reinforce anxiety in our lives. Specifically, *anxiety begets anxiety.*

There is more to thinking than thinking. Dr. Caroline Leaf, author of *Switch on your Brain,* reveals that our thinking is primarily a bodily function. Thinking is organic and biochemical.

Thinking sends neurological signals throughout our body: thinking influences our brain chemistry and our bodies, along with our mental, emotional, and spiritual health.

Some of my exposed faulty thoughts and beliefs:

I need to please people.
I need to be in control.
I need to be right.
I shouldn't be angry.

What are some of your faulty thoughts and beliefs? Where do they come from?

FIRST THOUGHTS

Our first thoughts are especially significant and insightful. Take a moment to unmask possible anxious thinking in your life. Be honest about it.

In the following scenarios, what would your first thought be?

* Your boss, spouse or child says, "I need to talk to you as soon as possible!"
* You have had a severe headache for over three days.
* A client doesn't return an urgent phone call or email.
* It's 11.30 P.M., and your 16-year-old daughter is an hour late home from a party.

With these everyday scenarios, we can quickly become agitated and distracted with anxiety-generating first thoughts. It is natural for our first thought to be mildly anxious. Regardless, for many people, they can quickly challenge their irrational first thought, become composed and move on.

Some of you may relate to my everyday scenario. On many occasions, *my first thoughts become consuming thoughts.* Anxiety begets anxiety.

Regrettably, I would spend hours (often at night) continuously replaying disastrous, exaggerated, and disturbing scenarios in my impressionable mind. There is no doubt that tomorrow looks like the words we think and speak today.

If you recognise anxious thinking patterns in your life, the good news is that like me—you can change the way you think. Over time and with regular practice, you can re-program or re-condition your mind to new and healthier thinking patterns.

RENEWAL

Some of my favourite words in the English language are "re" prefix words (words that begin with the letters "re"). The "re" prefix means "back" or "again."

Here are some examples:

- Refresh: *be made fresh again.*
- Refocus: *put back into focus.*
- Reignite: *to again be ignited with passion.*
- Renew: *make new again.*

Life is not static. Life is fluid. If you're feeling *stuck in shame,* then you can get unstuck. Today is a new day and an opportunity for a fresh start.

The Apostle Paul wrote from personal experience, "Do not conform any longer to the pattern of this world, but *be transformed by the renewing of your mind.*" [Romans 12:2, italics mine]

God's deep and, at times, hidden transformational work occurs through the renewing of our mind. Biblically speaking, however, to renew is not to restore my thinking to the old Rob, but to think like a *brand-new Rob.*

To renew our mind is to intentionally and radically change the way we think to the way God thinks. In other words, I am who God says I am, and I can do what God says I can do.

As Christ-followers, we are called by God to be holy nonconformists—to think differently from the world because we have the "mind of Christ" [1 Corinthians 2:16].

A new way of thinking leads to a new way of living. And one of the primary times the Holy Spirit will mysteriously and miraculously renew our mind is when we read and meditate on God's Word. After all, God's deep thoughts are revealed within the pages of His Holy Scriptures. Simply stated, *what is written is what I think*.

On page 167 there are examples of Scripture we can meditate on and activate the radical renewing of our mind.

CHANGE YOUR BRAIN

"Neuroplasticity is God's design for renewing the mind." —**Dr. Caroline Leaf**

Through the advances of neuroscience, we now understand that our brain is neuroplastic; i.e., our brain is pliable and adaptable. Be assured, we are not victims of difficult circumstances or our parents' rogue genes. We can change the way we think, change our brain, and change our lives.

Keep in mind, renewal is a process, and we need to embrace and trust the process, rather than continually seeking the "quick fix" or "zap moments."

Please understand, if shame can be turned on, then shame can be turned off. If shame can get on you, then shame can get off you.

Today, make up your mind to renew your mind.

Today, agree that toxic thinking has dominated and damaged your life for far too long.

Enough of saying, "I'm not good enough."

Enough of saying, "I'm not smart enough."

Enough of saying, "I'm not strong enough."

Enough of saying, "I'm not spiritual enough."

ENOUGH!

MIND GYM

Catch your thoughts

Apparently, we have an estimated 60,000 thoughts per day. Now that's a lot of thinking. What percentage of your daily 60,000 thoughts are toxic to your soul?

Below are some examples of toxic thinking:

Pessimistic

I can't cope.
I could never do that.
Nothing good ever happens to me.
I'm not good enough.

Fearful

What if I fail?
What if I get hurt?
What will people think?
Be careful.

Catastrophic

I'm going to die.
I will never get better.
Nobody cares.
This job is killing me.

Judgmental

God doesn't answer my prayers.
Everyone is against me.
I'm not good at anything.
I deserve better than this.

For decades, my top three daily anxious thoughts were:

I can't cope!
I don't have what it takes!
What will people think?

THINKING INVENTORY

1. For a moment, imagine you're a fisherman casting out a net into the expansive lake of your everyday thoughts. What would be your *catch of the day?*

2. Now, take the time to think about what you're thinking about. For a month, take an inventory of your daily thoughts. What do you think about most consistently? Write your thoughts down in an exercise book, computer or smartphone.

Complete this sentence: *My most repetitive and impacting toxic thought is* _____
_____
_____
_____

Challenge your thoughts
On my journey out of debilitating shame, I soon realised I couldn't afford to be passive and merely accept my anxious thoughts. Incidentally, we don't have to believe every thought that goes through our heads.

As we catch our anxious thoughts, we should be proactive and intentionally challenge our thoughts before they can be changed. Remember, anxious thinking is often irrational and exaggerated.

This is the time and place we need to take responsibility for our anxiety and act accordingly. We have a choice when it comes to our thinking.

Earlier in this chapter, you caught a repetitive and impacting toxic thought.

Where did your toxic thought come from? _____

_____

_____

How has your toxic thought been serving you? _____

_____

_____

Here are three "thinking challenges" that I have found particularly useful:

1. **Where is the evidence?**

   Don't make assumptions based on one aspect of a difficult situation. Learn to demand and seek all the facts.

   Examples: Where is the evidence that you are worthless or insignificant? Maybe your friend didn't return your email because they're sick, on holidays, their computer crashed, or your email has gone to their spam folder.

2. **What is the worst-case scenario?**

   Put your anxious thoughts into perspective. For example, with a panic attack, the worst scenario is you may faint. I have had hundreds of panic attacks and have never fainted. Even if I did faint—so what?

3. **Is the thought helpful?**

   Are your looping thoughts Biblical, truthful, and helpful? How are your thoughts serving you? How are your thoughts helping you fulfil your life purpose?

THINKING INVENTORY (cont.)

Change your thoughts

It's time to take ownership of our thinking and learn how to think for a change—a positive change! To be honest, changing years of habitual and anxious thinking hasn't come easy. To this day, if I'm not careful, under severe stress, I can easily default back to old and toxic thinking patterns.

Change involves courage and discipline over an extended period of time. We understand that exercise and diet entail discipline.

Until now, have you ever considered the discipline necessary to renew your thinking?

We urgently need to go on a diet for our thinking. Not a crash diet, where we don't think at all.

Now is the time to go on a "thinking detox."

Specifically, starve your toxic thoughts and regularly consume positive, life-giving thoughts.

Examples:

- *I am a child of God.* [Romans 8:16]
- *I am exceptionally gifted.* [1 Corinthians 12:7]
- *I am being renewed day by day.* [2 Corinthians 4:16]
- *I am a new creation.* [2 Corinthians 5:17]
- *I am blessed with every spiritual blessing.* [Ephesians 1:3]

- ✖ *I am loved affectionately by God.* [Ephesians 2:4]
- ✖ *I am seated with Christ in heavenly places.* [Ephesians 2:6]
- ✖ *I am never alone.* [Hebrews 13:5]
- ✖ *I am filled with an inexpressible and glorious joy.* [1 Peter 1:8]
- ✖ *I am completely forgiven.* [1 John 1:9]
- ✖ *I am filled with the Spirit of God.* [1 John 4:13]

Don't be alarmed or surprised if you have *toxic thinking withdrawals.* It is no different than experiencing withdrawals when you eliminate caffeine or sugar from your diet. Ultimately, your mind has been fed an unhealthy diet of toxic thinking for years.

Remember, what we focus on we strengthen. Focus on healthy, life-giving thoughts. Over time, those new thoughts will be strengthened and reinforced in your life.

The reality is, sometimes discipline or "trying harder" is not enough. If I were to say, "Don't think of a pink elephant," chances are you would think of a pink elephant. Right? There have been times when well-meaning phrases from our friends like "Don't be afraid" or "Stop thinking negative thoughts" don't cut it.

THE SILLY VOICE EXPERIMENT

Let me offer another technique to experiment with and experience. Australian psychotherapist and author Dr Russ Harris offers a refreshing perspective from his perceptive book, *The Happiness Trap* [p 64-68].

Even though no method is infallible, what Dr Russ recommends is a comical tactic for people who struggle to stop thinking an unpleasant thought.

He suggests we stop struggling to resist a repetitive toxic thought and merely change the sound of the voice. Imagine next time a toxic thought comes to mind, you immediately change the voice to:

* *Mickey Mouse*
* *Kermit the Frog*
* *Marge Simpson*
* *Mr Bean*
* *Rocky Balboa*

For example, with my repetitive toxic thought, "I can't cope," I now imagine Rocky doing push-ups at his boxing gym in Philadelphia. Yet, after only fifteen reps he cries out to his manager, Mickey (Burgess Meredith), "It's too hard Mickey! I can't cope!"

What I have recently discovered is that a comical change in tone can defuse the toxicity of the words I speak about myself to myself. The unpleasant thoughts may still come to mind, but they are hard to take seriously and are less intimidating.

What is your most repetitive toxic thought? _____

_____
_____
_____
_____
_____
_____
_____
_____

Choose a comical character and repeat several times
your toxic thought with their voice. _____

_____
_____
_____
_____
_____
_____
_____

Repeat this voice-over exercise for several weeks.
What's happening now? Is there a change of
emotion when you hear their silly voice? _____

_____
_____
_____
_____
_____
_____
_____

I'M STILL STANDING

Shame is a posture. Over recent years I have been learning to stand and walk with a posture of confidence and strength, even if I feel weak on the inside.

Challenging and changing my thinking has been a key to this transformation. It's time to take a stand of defiance in anticipation of our healing and breakthrough.

The recovery plan is straightforward—you must get up one more time than you fall. If you fall seven times, get up eight. [See Proverbs 24:16]

Take a stand against shame.

Put this book down and spend a few moments standing.

Stand tall.
Shoulders back and body straight.
Stand defiant.
Stand in faith.

Take a few deep breaths, smile, and declare:

I will not be shaken.
I will not be moved.
I'm still standing.

FURTHER THOUGHT AND CONTEMPLATION

Take a few minutes to be still and ponder these words from philosopher, playwright, novelist, and political activist Jean-Paul Sartre:

"Shame is a haemorrhage of the soul."

shame is a thief

"God gives us something better than a list of
answers; He gives us Himself."
—Joni Eareckson Tada

For decades, Hollywood has glamorised crime and entertained us through epic heist and robbery movies such as:

- *Butch Cassidy and the Sundance Kid* (1969)
- *The Italian Job* (1969, 2003)
- *The Sting* (1973)
- *Point Break* (1991, 2015)
- *Heat* (1995)
- *Entrapment* (1999)
- *Ocean's Trilogy* (2001, 2004, 2007)
- *Fast and Furious 5* (2011)

The first time something precious was stolen from me was
when I was in primary school. During the lunch break, the
boys either played British Bulldog or marbles. You might
have to Google the two games if you weren't in school during the 1960s or '70s.

During one lunch break, the boys were playing marbles.
I was watching a friend play a game and noticed he surprisingly had the exact coloured and patterned marbles as me.

Yes, marbles were unique, and most boys memorised their marble collection within their cherished marble bag.

Out of curiosity and suspicion, I immediately went to the classroom and looked through my school bag. Sure enough, my so-called friend had stolen all my marbles. With anger and resentment in my heart, I informed my teacher. Disappointingly, she sharply told me to stop whining and get over it. Oh, the injustice of it all—"I've lost my marbles!"

Shame is a thief. Shame can mercilessly rob us of sleep, inner peace, intimate relationships, confidence, and enjoyment. It's ironic that many of the activities I enjoy and find refreshing, such as surfing, eating out, going to the movies, and flying, have all been callously compromised by panic attacks.

As panic attacks increased and intensified, I have been repeatedly and ruthlessly robbed. Shame and my mental health struggles have robbed me and hindered my ability to engage in life fully. Can anyone relate to that?

MAYDAY

One example of shame robbing me of confidence was in May 2008. A little over fifteen months after my first panic attack, I continued to feel overwhelmed and agitated by the escalating demands and complexities of leading a growing church.

Even though church growth was positive, I was frustrated and humiliated by my inability to manage stress effectively. Over the coming months, I came to a point where I lost confidence in my calling and capacity to be a competent pastor. My journal entry on a particularly dark day during May was one dramatic word—"MAYDAY."

A couple of weeks later, during my faith and ministry crisis, I went to a friend's retreat centre in Toodyay, a charming historical town located in the Perth Hills. Before me was a fantastic opportunity for two days of solitude, reading, praying, contemplating, and walking in the bush.

After a two-hour drive, I unpacked my bag and made my bed. Then I had a brief and honest conversation with God. I was crying out to God: *I need help. I'm so broken. I desperately need a breakthrough. I need a fresh revelation.*

Ultimately, I was professing to God that I can't go back into ministry unless something dramatic happened, and it needed to happen right at that moment.

To get in the mood, I played some relaxing music. I didn't feel like listening to "happy clappy" worship music. Subsequently, I played a CD I hadn't heard for a couple of years—the melancholic sound of American musician and worship leader, Kevin Prosch.

The music took me back to a pleasant season when Karen and I attended the live recording of Prosch's worship album, in 1993, at the Anaheim Vineyard in southern California. After about seventy minutes, the last song began to play. The song is entitled, *A Song for Brent* and is a brilliant interpretation of Psalm 23.

I wasn't trying to make anything happen, I was simply still, attentive, and mildly expectant. A repetitive phrase, accompanied by a beautiful melody, captured my heart and imagination: *He restores my soul, He restores my soul, He restores my soul …*

That's all I needed to know. Over the two-day retreat, I was overwhelmed, not with fear and anxiety, but with the quiet assurance that God is and will continue to restore my tortured and hemorrhaging soul.

In that sacred space, I could hear another voice speaking deeply into my heart. The words from the *Father of Truth* were becoming louder and more penetrating than the words of the *father of lies*. The phrase, "He restores my soul" was louder and far more potent than "Shame on you!"

During the retreat, I took responsibility for my pain and anguish. I repented for the unyielding self-life, such as self-absorption, self-reliance, self-pity, and self-protection. One significant lesson I learnt was God's agenda wasn't to change my circumstances, but to supernaturally change me from the inside out.

FLYING HIGH

There have also been times when shame has robbed me of joy and the simple pleasures of life. Family holidays during January have become an important tradition for the Mason tribe. There are times when we stay at home and go on day trips to the local beach, museum or the movies. Other years we would spend a week down south in tranquil places like Dunsborough and Yallingup, in the stunning South West of Western Australia.

With another year of fruitful, yet demanding, ministry behind us, we were in for a treat—ten days on the glorious Gold Coast in Queensland. Apart from brilliant beaches, spectacular high-rise apartments and remarkable restaurants, there are the adrenaline-pumping theme parks such as *Movie World* and *Dream World*.

In early January 2010, we were flying to Brisbane with great expectations of another refreshing and fun-filled family holiday. We were about thirty minutes from landing, and it was time for a quick toilet break in the tiny cubicle at the back of the plane. Without notice, we hit mild turbulence, and I was getting jolted inside the toilet cubicle. My first thought was, *I bet my family is having a good laugh at me.* I was in a chilled mood, relaxed, and looking forward to having family fun on the Gold Coast.

As I made my way back to my seat and without warning, my heart rate escalated dramatically, and I was besieged with fear. I hadn't had a panic attack for over twelve months, and I couldn't believe I was having a major panic attack in a plane. Amy is back, and working tirelessly to protect me.

In the past, if I couldn't control or cope with a panic attack, I would leave. My worst fear was now my disturbing reality—I was trapped in a plane at 10,000 metres!

Thankfully, I didn't make a spectacle of myself, and I managed to control my breathing and panic. We landed, picked up our luggage, and hired a car. While driving to our hotel, my body was recovering from the intense panic attack—it felt like I was driving under the influence of drugs and alcohol. The reality was I was once again intoxicated with overwhelming amounts of adrenaline, norepinephrine, and cortisol.

On the first morning, I went for a leisurely walk along the beach of Surfers Paradise. However, after about fifteen minutes I looked back to our hotel, and I felt severe dread that compelled me to return quickly. It was yet another "walk of shame."

During our Gold Coast getaway, I didn't hire a surfboard, because of the fear of having a panic attack in the surf. Once again, shame has been a thief with a demising posture of despair and humiliation.

Over the next ten days, we went to a couple of the popular theme parks, and I did my best to appear "normal" in front of the kids and go on the wild rides with them. The last thing I needed, was more adrenaline pulsating through my body.

There was nonetheless times Karen took Emily and Jake out to the shops or lunch without me. To avoid the further humiliation of panic attacks, I preferred to stay alone within the safety of our hotel room. Amy was pleased with my cooperation.

The consuming thought during my holiday was the dread of flying back to Perth. What if it happens again? I contemplated two choices—either I need to take some strong medication before I fly back to Perth or I will have to catch the train home instead.

To fly home takes five hours; to travel by train takes about sixty-five hours. You would think my choice was a no-brainer. By the way, when you're in a constant state of intense panic, logic is not a factor to consider. Your number one priority is survival.

When Amy is activated, the area of our brain responsible for problem-solving and decision-making is temporarily dismissed.

The other disturbing and more confronting questions were:

Why haven't I been healed?

Am I finally disqualified from ministry?

THE PAIN OF SHAME

It would now be advantageous to unpack and break down the shame of my mental health struggle. As I look back over the past decade, this is what has specifically fueled my shame:

- **I was ashamed of feeling overwhelmed.** I was ashamed of my inability to cope with and manage stress. I was ashamed that my life was spiralling out of control and I had been unmasked as weak and incompetent.

- **I was ashamed of panic.** I was ashamed that my life had been dominated and impacted by something that was invisible and people didn't fully understand and empathise with.

- **I was ashamed of insomnia, fatigue, and low libido.** I was ashamed of how anxiety, panic, and shame had impacted my physical, emotional, and spiritual wellbeing and close relationships. I was ashamed of how I had let my family and church down on several occasions, because of crippling despair and fatigue.

- **I was ashamed of avoidance.** I was ashamed of avoiding places like shopping centres, the dentist, or public transport because I was afraid of having another public panic attack. I was ashamed, confused, angry, and resentful that I had been robbed of confidence and joy.

- **I was ashamed of withdrawal.** I was ashamed of having to regularly leave the movies, a restaurant, or the surf, because I felt a panic attack coming on, and I was unable to manage my breathing.

- **I was ashamed of going on a mental health plan, receiving therapy, and taking medication.** What more can I say? I falsely believed at the time that this was a sign of weakness rather than being courageously vulnerable. And, finally,

- **I was ashamed of my shame.** As you can appreciate, shame is complicated, chaotic, and compounding. Shame begets shame, begets shame.

Shame is extremely painful and can become all-consuming. Even so, keep reading because the next two chapters reveal another aspect and dimension of shame.

THE SHAME AND FEAR CONNECTION

For a moment, let's go back to the beginning of time and the birth of the catastrophic shame narrative. Look and contemplate the following verses, if you want, circle the words "heard," "hid," "afraid" and "naked."

"Then the man and his wife heard the sound of the Lord God as He was walking in the garden in the cool of the day, and they hid from the Lord God among the trees of the garden.

But the Lord God called to the man, 'Where are you?'

He answered, 'I heard You in the garden, and I was afraid because I was naked; so I hid.'" [Genesis 3:8-10]

In the beginning, the glory of God consumed the Garden of Eden and covered the nakedness of Adam and Eve. Moments after they were deceived by the devil, they heard the approach of God.

Was that a familiar sound?

Did God regularly visit, walk with, and daily manifest a fresh revelation of His glory? If so, surely the sound of God approaching was both calming and reassuring.

Everything has dramatically and severely changed. For the first time in history, God's presence was a perceived threat.

Could it be that this is the first-time Amy or the amygdala was activated in the human brain?

The first Biblical record of fear was not Adam facing a 400-kg sabre-toothed tiger, but the terrifying sound of God's approach.

Our ancient ancestors were exposed and consumed with shame. At once they desperately covered their nakedness that was once pure, untainted, and innocent. Adam informs God they hid from His presence because they were spiritually and emotionally naked, ashamed, and afraid.

Can you see that shame and fear play off each other? Shame provokes fear and fear provokes shame. There is a mysterious collaboration between shame and fear. Together, they strengthen and reinforce each other as one intimidating force, within the vulnerable human soul.

From my first unpleasant memory of having an injection in a hospital to having a panic attack in a plane, there was indeed a lethal synergy of shame and fear.

When I experienced the shame of humiliation, failure, and fatherly neglect, fear instantly formed a memory of pain and danger within my pliable brain. Simultaneously, Amy stepped in and detected further perceived threats. When there's a ping on the radar, Amy releases stress hormones to prepare me for yet another *fight-freeze-flight* response.

From my understanding, when life becomes consumed with fear, anxiety, feeling overwhelmed, depression, and shame, your world becomes smaller and smaller. You ultimately and regrettably become consumed with *you* and managing *you*.

DEATH TO SELFIE

There is no doubt that we're living in a selfie world. So much so, that the Oxford Dictionary announced their Word of the Year for 2013 was "selfie."

A selfie is a picture taken "of yourself by yourself" using a smartphone. After applying a few apps such as filters to improve our looks, our astonishing selfie is displayed to a worldwide audience through social media [Facebook and Instagram].

The best selfies are those taken in famous places such as the Sydney Harbour Bridge, at a concert, a major sporting event, or with a high-profile celebrity. One of the most famous selfies ever taken was by host Ellen DeGeneres during the 86th Academy Awards in 2014, where she had over 2 million likes and over 3 million retweets [BBC News, 3 March 2014].

From where I stand, my mental health struggles were only symptoms of a far deeper issue—the "selfie-life." We are all born with a self-centred nature. The trinity of our brokenness is an obsession with me, myself, and I. The selfie-life does more damage to our hearts than high cholesterol.

The shame associated with our mental health struggles magnifies and compounds the selfie-life. For example, while attending a conference, rather than having the attitude and expectation of, *Who can I encourage today?* it was unfortunately replaced with, *Will I cope? Where are the exit signs if I should leave suddenly?*

Here is a selfie list from my struggle with shame and chronic anxiety:

- Self-consciousness: *what will people think?*
- Self-criticism: *what's wrong with me?*
- Self-pity: *what about me?*
- Self-protection: *how can I protect myself?*
- Self-reliance: *can I do it myself?*
- Self-blame: *what have I done to deserve this?*
- Self-rejection: *do I even belong here?*
- Self-gratification: *how can I numb my pain?*
- Self-deception: *am I hopeless?*
- Self-condemnation: *why do I hate my life?*

From my perspective, the only remedy to the destructive selfie-life is unconditional surrender. We often associate the word "surrender" with the bitter and humiliating resignation of defeat in war.

Jesus has rewritten the script of life and profoundly proclaimed a Kingdom paradox: *we find our life when we lose our life* [Matthew 10:39].

On another occasion, Jesus said to His disciples, "Self-help is no help at all. Self-sacrifice is the way, My way, to saving yourself, your true self." [Mark 8:35, MSG, italics mine]

For decades, my focus has been getting free from the shame of paralysing insecurity and unruly anxiety. Perhaps God's agenda all along is for me to be free from me or my "old self."

We don't need another "self-help" book to assist us in navigating through our shame and mental health struggles. What we do need is to *surrender our agenda* and seek "Jesus-help" to transform our broken lives.

THE DARK NIGHT OF THE SOUL

A Carmelite Monk, affectionately known John of the Cross, wrote a profound book while in prison during the 1500s entitled, *The Dark Night of the Soul.* He believed that with great anguish comes great insight. The dark night of the soul isn't necessarily punishment, but God is executing a deep and mysterious work within our private world.

John of the Cross said that if we're seeking hard after God and we also experience a prolonged time of spiritual barrenness, we shouldn't be alarmed because God is freeing us from ourselves.

One insight through my difficult journey with chronic anxiety is the opportunity to get over myself; I need to be saved from me.

Like many of you, I have been longing for a breakthrough—a time when all my pain and turmoil has finally gone. In hindsight and by God's grace, I can honestly testify that *my breakdown has been my breakthrough.*

It's taken several years, but I can honestly say I am grateful for my first public panic attack back in 2007. It was a devastating experience and yet at the same time—mysteriously liberating.

One life lesson I have slowly gleaned through my journey with the shame of chronic anxiety is it's impossible to be consumed with self and God at the same time.

Allow author, speaker, and contemplative Brennan Manning to explain: "Self-absorption fades into self-forgetfulness, as we fix our gaze on the brightness of the Lord." [Ruthless Trust, p 93]

It's time for Death to Selfie.

It's time to welcome the blessedness of self-forgetfulness.

It's time to renew our passionate gaze upon the glory of God:

"O God, You are my God;
earnestly I seek You;
my soul thirsts for You;
my flesh faints for You,
as in a dry and weary land
where there is no water."

[Psalm 63:1, ESV]

WELLBEING CHECK UP

Place a tick in the appropriate boxes.

	Empty tank	Low tank	Half tank	Full tank
Spiritual				
Emotional				
Physical				
Relational				
Intellectual				
Vocational				

Which area has the lowest reading? _____

_____

_____

_____

What are the signs when you're running on empty?

_____

_____

_____

_____

What is one thing you could do to fill your tank? ___

_____

_____

_____

_____

FURTHER THOUGHT AND CONTEMPLATION

Right here, right now, you have this valuable time to think about God. Once you feel still in God's presence, read Matthew 11:28-30 from *The Message* slowly and reflectively a couple of times. Read with the expectation that God will speak to you and guide your thoughts.

"Are you tired? Worn out? Burned out on religion? Come to Me. Get away with Me and you will recover your life. I'll show you how to take a real rest. Walk with Me and work with Me—watch how I do it. Learn the unforced rhythms of grace. I won't lay anything heavy or ill-fitting on you. Keep company with Me and you will learn to live freely and lightly."

Which word or phrase speaks deeply into your soul? Why?

_____

_____

_____

Now turn Matthew 11:28-30 into prayer or intimate conversation with God. This is an ancient spiritual practice called, *lectio divina* [sacred reading].

shame is a connection

"Pain is the common ground God gives us to
meet people." —**Dave Gibbons**

This chapter graciously reveals a remarkable turning point
in my shame narrative. There is another layer, facet, and perspective of shame to ponder.

When all is said and done, the pain of shame is our connection with broken humanity. Every person on planet earth
has and is experiencing shame at some level. You could say
that shame is the great equaliser of humanity—we are all
in the same boat. Shame and brokenness is our common
ground.

Yet that raises the question—why do we hide our shame
when it's the common mark of humanity? Through twenty-seven years of pastoral ministry, I have discovered surprisingly that most people relate more to my weaknesses
than my strengths. Yet for a substantial part of ministry,
I was foolishly attempting to convince people that I am
strong and competent. Go figure.

Every person longs to be part of an authentic community—*we long to belong*. Ironically, one of the things that
unites us is our scars. Before people witness our miraculous

healing and recovery, they will first observe our patience and perseverance through the pain of our chronic brokenness.

There are possibly people right now watching you wrestle with the shame of your mental health struggles—not to judge you, but to learn from you and be inspired by you.

Our scars make us relevant and relatable. Our scars are stories that are both vulnerable and empowering. My counsel is simple—let us no longer be afraid to show each other our scars of shame and brokenness.

JARS OF CLAY

"But we have this treasure in jars of clay to show that this all-surpassing power is from God and not from us." [2 Corinthians 4:7]

"We now have this light shining in our hearts, but we ourselves are like fragile clay jars containing this great treasure. This makes it clear that our great power is from God, not from ourselves." [NLT]

It has taken me a long time to resolve, but perception is no longer my preferred reality. *Divine revelation is my new and preferred reality.* These ancient and sacred words from the Apostle Paul, present a compelling insight into my new identity "in Christ."

Yes, like every other human on the planet I am a weak, fragile, and broken vessel. I am a "cracked pot." For the past six chapters, I have shared my shame narrative with you. On the contrary, there is a superior and eternal reality.

We are jars of clay, yet at the same time, we are graciously and supernaturally infused with the light or radiance of God's power and goodness.

Paul reveals the nature of this remarkable treasure in the

previous verse: "For God, who said, 'Let light shine out of darkness,' made His light shine in our hearts..." (6)

What is Paul up to?

Why does Paul include a reference to the creation of light from Genesis 1:3?

Could it be that Paul is introducing the Genesis connection to reveal God's *new creation narrative?* Through Christ, we are a *new humanity* or jars of clay filled with the light of God's glory. Subsequently, we are fragmented, and fragile humans supernaturally pervaded with the empowering presence of God. Now that's worth getting excited about.

Likewise, within Japanese art, there is "wabi-sabi"—the capacity to discover beauty within imperfection and incompletion. An excellent example of wabi-sabi is seen in certain styles of Japanese pottery. The artist believes the flaws such as a chip or crack, is what makes the fashioned object beautiful. Put another way, *the flaws become the masterpiece.*

On the contrary, we strive to cover our flaws. What if God's intends to place our flaws on display as He executes an extraordinary work through us?

CRIES OF THE HEART

Behind words such as "anxiety," "overwhelmed," "stress," "burnout," "discouragement," and "depression" is PAIN. Our pain and brokenness are what make us human.

The Bible is not silent about the dilemma of our pain and emotional turmoil. From cover to cover, we have an honest record about a diversity of people with great faith, who at the same time experienced anxiety, fear, stress, deep despondency, and depression. Nothing is swept under the carpet. The Bible is less sanitised and domesticated than we think.

How many of the following "cries of the heart" can you relate to? Why is their cry relatable to your life?

Adam: "I heard You in the garden, and I was afraid..." [Genesis 3:10]

Rachel: "So she said to Jacob, 'Give me children, or I'll die!'" [Genesis 30:1]

Moses: "I can't carry all these people by myself! The load is far too heavy! If this is how You intend to treat me, just go ahead and kill me. Do me a favour and spare me this misery!" [Numbers 11:14-15, NLT]

Elijah: "I have had enough, LORD, he said. Take my life; I am no better than my ancestors." [1 Kings 19:4]

Job: "Cursed be the day of my birth, and cursed be the night when I was conceived. Let that day be turned to darkness. Let it be lost even to God on high, and let it be shrouded in darkness." [Job 3:3-4, NLT]

David: "O LORD, why do you stand so far away? Why do you hide when I need you the most?" [Psalm 10:1, NLT]

Jeremiah: "I have cried until the tears no longer come. My heart is broken, my spirit poured out in agony, as I see the desperate plight of my people..." [Lamentations 2:11, NLT]

Jesus: "My soul is overwhelmed with sorrow to the point of death..." [Matthew 26:38]

MAN OF SORROWS

Pain connected Jesus to humanity. Jesus spent abundant amounts of His precious time with people suffering severely. Not surprisingly, untamed Jesus focused intentionally on the weak and vulnerable during His ministry on earth. Jesus connected intimately with the fragmented, forsaken, and forgotten.

Search the Gospels, and you will find Jesus with unclean lepers, despised tax collectors, marginalised sick, the oppressed poor, demonically-tormented, and the sexually-broken. Consequently, God is not removed from our pain; God feels our pain and is moved by our pain.

Jesus also experienced His own pain. For example, Jesus experienced the tragic loss of His earthly father Joseph and relative John the Baptist. Jesus felt firsthand the pain of thirst, hunger, weariness, disappointment, ridicule, abandonment, betrayal, torture, and death.

The Roman Empire during the first century perfected the ancient and barbaric form of torture through the crucifixion. They experimented with their victims over decades to discover how to inflict maximum pain and tormenting shame.

Think for a moment about the crucifixion of Jesus. For six excruciating hours, Jesus experienced unimaginable pain and unparalleled vulnerability.

These appalling methods of pain and shame included:

1. Spitting at Jesus
   In ancient middle eastern times, spitting at or on someone was one of the fervent signs of disgust and disrespect [Job 30:10]. In certain situations, under Mosaic Law, to

be spat upon meant you were ceremonially unclean and quarantined from the faith community for seven days [Numbers 12:14].

Both Roman soldiers [Matthew 26:67] and numerous Jewish religious leaders spat on Jesus during His unjust and heartless interrogation [Matthew 27:30]. There is the possibility that Jesus' face was dripping with human saliva from malicious men in authority who despised Him.

That humiliating insult was a fulfilment of an ancient prophecy concerning Jesus before His crucifixion: "I did not hide My face from mocking and spitting." [Isaiah 50:6]

2. Striking Jesus

Fortunately, I've only been punched in the face twice in my life. The first incident occurred when I was about ten years old while walking home with my sister Sue. A teenage guy, whom I'd never seen before, was riding a bike and asked me if my name was Rob Mason. When I answered yes, he abruptly got off his bike and punched me in my mouth. I have no idea why he punched me— maybe there was another Rob Mason who lived in Doonside?

Apart from the pain of my cut lip, the experience of being punched and crying in front of my younger sister was also humiliating. That incident diminishes into insignificance when we contemplate Jesus' experience.

The soldiers not only spat on Jesus, but they also violently struck or slapped Jesus in the head repeatedly [Matthew 27:30]. There was even a time Jesus was blindfolded and punched, then asked to prophesy who was responsible [Mark 14:65].

3. Stripping off Jesus' clothes

Roman crucifixions intentionally imposed the nakedness of their victims. There is nothing more vulnerable and humiliating than being tortured naked in public.

Before Jesus was scourged (flogged), the Roman soldiers stripped Jesus' garments off and placed a scarlet (colour of royalty) robe on Him [Matthew 27:28, 31]. Think about this—Jesus didn't change His clothing in the privacy of a changing room.

Jesus was denied dignity—He was publically stripped, and a mock robe and crown were placed on a perceived mock king, to add to His public humiliation.

We also read that some of the Roman guards cast lots for the garments of Jesus while He was dying on the cross [Matthew 27:35; John 19:23-24].

Even if the Roman soldiers permitted Jesus to wear a loin cloth or undergarment, this was still exceedingly humiliating for a Jewish man living in the modest first century.

4. Scorning Jesus

Throughout Jesus' trial, interrogation, and crucifixion, the Jewish and Roman officials continually scorned Jesus [Matthew 27:27-44]. To scorn is to ridicule, disdain, belittle, and humiliate the victim.

Examples of scorning:

- "Hail, King of the Jews!" (29)
- "If You are the Son of God, come down from the cross." (40)
- "He saved others; He cannot save Himself." (42)

[Adapted from Neyrey, J. H. *Despising the Shame of the Cross: Honor and Shame in the Johannine Passion Narrative.* Semeia 69 (1996):113-37]

SCORNING SHAME

With the drama of the cross in mind, ponder the profound words from the unknown writer to the Jewish Christian community: "Let us fix our eyes on Jesus, the author and perfecter of our faith, who for the joy set before Him endured the cross, *scorning its shame...*" [Hebrews 12:2, italics mine]

Slow down for a moment and chew on these words: Jesus vehemently scorned the shame of the cross, while on the cross.

What else took place on the "old rugged cross?"
Jesus was unmoved by shame.
Jesus humiliated shame.
Jesus disarmed shame.
Jesus forced shame to hide.
Jesus silenced shame.
Jesus put shame to shame.

On the cross, shame was fittingly covered with shame. The host of shame was not the vulnerable soul of Jesus—the host of shame was shame.

A NEW COVERING

"The Lord God made garments of skin for Adam and his wife and *clothed them.*" [Genesis 3:21, italics mine]

Before God justifiably banished Adam and Eve from the Garden of Eden, He tenderly clothed them. To be clothed with "garments of skin" implies an animal sacrifice. Adam and Eve's covering through the shedding of blood is the first Biblical and prophetic reference of redemption and atonement [at-one-ment]. The Hebrew word "atonement" (*kopher*) is one of the richest theological words in the Old Testament. Through atonement, sin is removed, cancelled, cleansed, and disarmed. Ironically, one of the other meanings of atonement is "to cover."

Throughout the sacred Torah (the first five books of Moses) stands a myriad of covering imagery:

* *The covering of sin and blood*
  "For the life of a creature is in the blood, and I have given it to you to make atonement for yourselves on the altar; it is the blood that makes atonement for one's life." [Leviticus 17:11]

* *The covering of the Ark of the Covenant*
  "I will meet with you there and talk to you from above the atonement cover between the gold cherubim that hover over the Ark of the Covenant." [Exodus 25:22, NLT]

* *The covering of God's hand*
  "When My glory passes by, I will put you in a cleft in the rock and cover you with My hand until I have passed by." [Exodus 33:22]

* *The covering of the tabernacle*
  "Make for the tent a covering of ram skins dyed red, and over that a covering of the other durable leather." [Exodus 26:14]

* *The covering of God's glory*
  "Then the cloud covered the tent of meeting, and the glory of the LORD filled the tabernacle." [Exodus 40:34]

In contrast to God's majestic covering of righteousness, the Bible reveals that our righteous deeds and heart are "filthy garments" or "filthy rags" [Isaiah 64:6].

Astonishingly, by grace alone, through faith alone, in Christ alone, we are magnificently clothed and covered with the righteousness of God [Isaiah 61:10; Zechariah 3:3-4; Galatians 3:26-27; 2 Corinthians 5:21].

Through the nakedness and vulnerability of Jesus on the cross, we have a new garment available to cover our sin and shame. We are mercifully and eternally covered.

Repeat these words several times: *I am covered in Christ…*

A NEW NARRATIVE

Our new covering offers a new narrative. The unrelenting shame of my mental health has been devastating and, at times, humiliating. But the reality is there has always been a gracious invitation offered by God—come as you are, not as you want to be.

Many of us have responded to a position vacant advertisement in the newspaper or online. The advert specifies the necessary qualifications such as education, experience, skills, and character.

This begs the question—who qualifies for grace? The answer is any person who humbly acknowledges their sin (weaknesses) and surrenders their selfie-life to Jesus. Through the onslaught of modern life, the grace recipients concede they are spiritually bankrupt and desperately need God for salvation.

Through the turmoil of my mental health, I have been regularly reminded of my weakness and brokenness. Over the past few years, I have become more overwhelmed by God's outrageous grace than my contemptable shame. That, my friends, is my advantage in life, and it can be yours too.

From now on, the only weight we carry in life is the weight of God's glory and grace. Unlike shame, the weight of grace is light, comfortable, and calming.

You may be familiar with the phrase "fall from grace." We often apply it to people in authority (politicians, pastors, and priests) or people of influence (celebrities and sporting heroes). When they have publically failed, ethically or morally, they lose our respect and support.

What should be music to our ears, is in God's Kingdom we don't fall from grace; instead, *we fall into grace*—over and over again.

THE GRACE NARRATIVE

The Bible is not only a narrative about shame, but the Bible is also a narrative about God's amazing and enriching grace.

Before we put on our new covering, we first courageously remove our inferior and temporary covering. As I said in a previous chapter, like Adam and Eve, we hide our shame on our terms and using our methods; such as busyness, entertainment, and addictions.

Once our old coverings are removed and we are naked or vulnerable before God, we can audaciously put on the covering of Christ. As we put on the covering of Jesus, we embrace, trust, and focus on His sufficiency, not our insufficiency.

Remember, shame feeds on hiddenness. Through the covering of Christ, God has given me the grace and courage to tell my story—to be seen and heard.

Today, I joyfully embrace vulnerability and speak openly about my journey with shame and chronic anxiety through preaching, writing, and mentoring. Collectively, they break the silence of shame and force shame to hide.

The bottom line is—through Christ, we are covered.

There is no reason anymore to hide and cover-up our naked soul.

I am forever grateful for the unshakable truth—*Where shame abounds, grace abounds more.*

Shame doesn't have the last word in my life—grace has the last word.

There is always more grace than shame.

My parting words from this chapter are:

Shame off you and GRACE ON YOU!

FIVE SENSES

Mindfulness is a brilliant and beneficial stress-reduction technique. To be mindful is to be attentive, curious, and in the present moment.

Begin this exercise by sitting comfortably.

Spend a few minutes focusing on deep belly breathing.

When you feel relaxed, slowly and attentively activate your five senses.

1. Notice five things you can see.

2. Notice four things you can touch.

3. Notice three things you can hear.

4. Notice two things you can smell.

5. Notice one thing you can taste.

[Adapted from *Five Senses Mindfulness Exercise*, Clayton State University, Counseling and Psychological Services, USA]

FURTHER THOUGHT AND CONTEMPLATION

Through reading this book, what is one thing you have learnt about:

Your shame _____

_____

_____

_____

Your mental health _____

_____

_____

_____

Your faith _____

_____

_____

_____

PERSONAL NOTES

8

shame is a pathway

"A bird doesn't sing because it has an answer, it sings because it has a song!" —**Joan Augland**

Shame is a pathway. Shame is not static or stagnant—it always leads you somewhere. The "shame pathway" is perilous and unpredictable. Along this pathway are hidden potholes, hairpin corners, and deep ravines that can execute untold damage to our soul.

There was a period in my life when shame was a perilous pathway that led directly and ruthlessly to my mental health struggles.

As I said in the prologue, I was confronted with a "shame double-whammy." Shame was a pathway to my mental health struggle, and my mental health struggle was a pathway to intensified and compounding shame. I understand the shame of our mental health struggles can cause us to be bitter and resentful.

The good news is there is an alternative route or pathway of shame. This may come as a shock to some of you, but shame has the potential to be a pathway to God's enriching grace.

What is grace?

One facet of grace is it's God's empowering presence.

The ageless guideposts in the Bible indicate to the "faith pilgrim" of an alternative pathway that is unexpected, undeserved, and absolutely brilliant.

RED CROSS

At the beginning of this book, I revealed my first conscious experience of fear and humiliation was during day surgery as a four-year-old boy. Fear is a memory of danger, and for decades I was distressed by my fear of needles.

In 1984, I was preparing to be a local church pastor at a theological college in Sydney. Within a couple of months, I discovered that one of my colleagues was a pathologist. Up until that point people like doctors, nurses, and pathologists were my enemies and a threat of imminent danger. I have provided Amy with ample data to reinforce her desire to protect me.

During a break between lectures, I took a risk and openly shared with the female pathologist my lifelong and consuming fear of needles. She firstly reassured me that I'm not alone. From her experience as a seasoned pathologist, the two groups of people who don't usually cope well with needles are children and men.

Men?

What a relief.

I'm not the only man on planet earth afraid of needles.

Her next step in my desensitisation was she provided me with a syringe to take to my room at college. For several days, that horrid and tormenting syringe sat on my desk with my Bible, college textbooks, and stationery.

The syringe on my desk was gradually becoming a

familiar sight. I would even walk pass the syringe and talk to it: "Hello you instrument of terror. It's all your fault. You suck."

Over time I gathered the courage to remove the plastic cap off the syringe and gently touch the sharp needle with my finger. The next step was to take the cap off and touch the vein of my arm with the needle as if I'm about to have a blood test. So far, so good.

My next challenge in overcoming my fear was to go to my friendly pathologist's bedroom at college and allow her to have the syringe and touch my arm. In other words, I'm no longer in control, and that has been one of my underlying issues in life. She was always asking if I was okay and reassured me that I was doing well.

Finally, she asked the dreaded question, "Are you ready for your first blood test?" After a prolonged moment of being typically indecisive, I reluctantly and softly said "Yes." While closing my eyes and with my body tense, I encountered my first blood test.

Not surprisingly, all I felt was a slight sting, and it was all over. *That's it.* I thought to myself. I was both relieved and embarrassed that I allowed a syringe to dominate my life with fear.

My friend Amy had a lot of explaining to do. To be fair, Amy was only doing her primal duty with the data I provided her over the years. Then again, Amy now had *new data from a new experience and a new memory.* Amy quickly adapted and learnt to detect that needles were not a threat, and she no longer had to change my physiology to prepare me for battle.

Now for the amusing and redemptive part of the story. A few weeks after my triumphant blood test, a few of my friends from college invited me to join them to donate blood at the local Red Cross. There was a time when such an appointment was inconceivable.

After completing some medical history forms and final instructions, I donated blood for the first time in my life. The reward (apart from the people who benefited from my precious blood donation) for my new-found bravery was a hotdog, chocolate bar, and orange juice for lunch. Not bad considering lunch at college five days per week was salad and cold meat.

Significantly, if fear is the memory of danger, then fear must also be a learned behaviour. If fear is a learned behaviour, then it's possible to unlearn a detrimental response to fear. Sure, you can't delete an old memory of fear, but *you can create a new memory*.

As we think new thoughts, we also miraculously create new neural pathways in our brain. Amy shouldn't be the solo voice in our brains and lives. As I said before, there is more to life than safety and survival.

My pathologist friend exercised what is known as "systematic desensitisation" or "exposure" to help me overcome my learned fear-response to needles.

Over the past thirty years and with minimal fuss, I have had a vasectomy, four wisdom teeth removed, four dental crowns inserted, two minor knee procedures, and several cysts surgically removed.

Amy is now uncharacteristically calm and quiet when it comes to needles.

DO IT AFRAID

Normally, how do you manage fear? A common but ineffective strategy is avoidance. When we sense a ping on Amy's danger detector, stress hormones are released, and we feel compelled to flee or avoid the situation.

Here are some everyday examples of avoidance:

- *You don't go in a lift.*
- *You don't fly in a plane.*
- *You don't meet new people.*
- *You don't get married.*
- *You don't go to the doctor or dentist.*
- *You don't speak in public.*
- *You don't swim in the ocean.*
- *You don't take risks.*

There is no growth or victory if we avoid our fear, ignore our fear, or run away from our fear. The alternative is—*do it afraid.***

1. What are you afraid of?
2. How does fear impact your life?
3. Conquer a small fear first.

Start by confronting a fear that is only mildly scary.

Slowly and repeatedly expose yourself to that fear.

As you progress and gain confidence, gently work your way up to face your greatest fear.

****Warning:** if the fear you confront is potentially dangerous (e.g. swimming in the ocean) ensure you have a companion with you.

ARE WE THERE YET?

One of our favourite family holiday destinations is the stunning South West region, a leisurely three-hour drive from Perth. It's such a great feeling to have the car packed, driving south with the city in the rear-view mirror.

When our kids were young, they loved the destination, but not the three-hour drive. After one hour, they began to whine in unison, "Are we there yet?" About halfway along the journey, they needed a refreshment break, to stretch their restless legs and decide on their preferred takeaway for lunch.

This is true for the journey of shame and our mental health struggles. We long for the destination of freedom from pain, inner peace, and restored emotional wellbeing. What's more, we can be like my kids in the back seat of the car moaning to God in unison, "Are we there yet?"

Before we go any further, let's spend a few moments unpacking the question, "Are we there yet?"

Where exactly is "there?"

Have you ever taken the time to ponder what "there" really looks like?

Why do you want to be "there" and not "here?"

What are you going to do when you get "there?"

How will life be different or better when you are "there?"

What if you're not ready for "there?"

Perhaps the reason you're not "there" yet is God's mercy.

Maybe something needs to first happen in you in the "here" before you're ready for the new opportunities and challenges of "there."

Let's now take some time and explore the journey of recovery and growth.

Here are a couple of my travelling tips:

1. Embrace the journey

If we want to experience healing, recovery, and breakthrough with our shame and mental health, then we must accept that change rarely happens overnight.

To progress from where we are today to where we desire to be in the future involves radical change, and change takes time. Momentous growth always takes longer than we expect.

Don't be deceived—small steps are not insignificant steps. Small steps equal progress. Small steps initiate movement, and movement leads to momentum. Along your journey, don't believe the shame lies:

Nothing will change.
You're stuck.
You're going backwards.
You're always going to feel this way.

Have you noticed that growth can be messy and gruelling? Remember puberty? Growth not only takes longer than we expect, but growth is usually more demanding than we imagine.

Why is growth painful? Growth may involve vulnerability, transparency, accountability, confession, forgiveness, setbacks, frustration, confusion, and a radical lifestyle change.

How many of us will do anything to avoid emotional pain? To move forward in life, we must weigh up the long-term consequences of avoiding our pain, versus the outcomes of embracing our pain.

Which pain do you prefer? The pain of avoidance or the pain of growth? Who knows, maybe a month without emotional pain is a month without growth. Read these ancient words attentively from French mystic Madame Jeanne Guyon: "If knowing answers to life's questions is absolutely necessary to you, then forget the journey. You will never make it, for this is a journey of unknowables— of unanswered questions, enigmas, incomprehensibles, and most of all, things unfair."

Did you take note of her prophetic perception and counsel? Forget the journey if you feel entitled to know the complexities of life's questions. At the end of the day, the critical issue is we can only embrace the journey if we firstly trust in God's goodness and sovereignty.

Along with our journey of faith and adventure, we will discover that God's ways are higher than our ways; God's thoughts are wiser than our thoughts, and God's timing is always superior to our timing. [See Isaiah 55:8-9]

2. Enjoy the journey

On our journey of healing and recovery, let's stop moaning and groaning to God, "Are we there yet?" or "That's not fair!" or "Why me?" or "What about me?" Let's change our attitude and learn to enjoy the journey of growth.

There are times we're so focused on our destination (healing, breakthrough, or dreams), we forget to enjoy the journey—the here and now. After all, *the journey is in the journey*. Life is more about the journey than the destination. It is time to enjoy the present moment—the "right here, right now" of life.

Even if we don't immediately see healing, or if growth is taking longer than expected or is harder than expected, be assured that God is always at work. Paul experienced excruciating pain and was qualified to write, "Therefore we do not lose heart. Though outwardly we are wasting away, yet inwardly we are being renewed day by day." [2 Corinthians 4:16]

Like me, your defining moments of dysfunction can also be your defining moments of growth and maturity. To be honest, I haven't arrived, I'm still vulnerable to chronic anxiety, I'm still on a journey, and I wouldn't have it any other way.

Listen to the words of Isaiah: "That's right. Because I, your GOD, have a firm grip on you and I'm not letting go. I'm telling you, *'Don't panic. I'm right here to help you.'*" [41:13, MSG, italics mine]

Shame is indeed a pathway. The pain of my shame has been a pathway from Shameville to Gracelands. In turn, shame is not the end, but the beginning.

Shame is the prelude or starting place of radical transformation.

Don't get stuck in your shame.

LETTER TO DAD

To this day, it is difficult to recall, but somewhere between the eighth and twelfth therapy session, the meeting took an unexpected and unusual twist. My assignment was to read out loud a letter addressed to my dad that I had written a fortnight before. Sounds straightforward. The intention of the letter was never to send it to Dad but to express my feelings on paper honestly.

What made the exercise even more intimidating was there was an empty chair in the office, and I had to pretend Dad was sitting in it while I read the letter. [Gestalt Therapy: The Empty Chair Technique]. Even though the letter was not being assessed, once again I had to let go of my fear of looking stupid and desire to be strong and in control.

There was an initial awkward moment, as I attempted to compose myself and clear my throat. In a moment, I was in the moment. I was reading the letter out loud, and it was as though my therapist wasn't present in the room. I was reading the letter before an invisible audience of two—my earthly father and my Heavenly Father.

For over thirty years I have preached, continually learning the art of effective communication and articulating my thoughts, beliefs, convictions, and emotions. In contrast, I was seated in the small, unassuming office of my therapist, my delivery unrefined and undignified, yet brutally real and honest. All the while, I was sobbing between sentences and wondering what my therapist was going to do with me.

THE DOMINO EFFECT

In the authenticity of another session, I received an unexpected revelation, but it was not from my therapist. God graciously imparted a truth that was straightforward, yet deeply profound—*I have always been fathered.*

To my surprise, I saw and heard the spectacle of cascading dominoes. All it took was one falling domino, to cause all the other dominos that were lined up also to fall. What's that all about? My interpretation of the "domino effect" was that one revelation from Heaven could release an unstoppable chain reaction of healing and restoration.

What were the other dominos? The other dominos were false and destructive thoughts about my dad and me. Straight away they were dismantled and disempowered by one domino or revelation—*I have always been fathered.*

Don't get me wrong. The supernatural revelation didn't mean therapy was no longer necessary, but I had a quiet, mystical confidence that my current emotional turmoil was temporary.

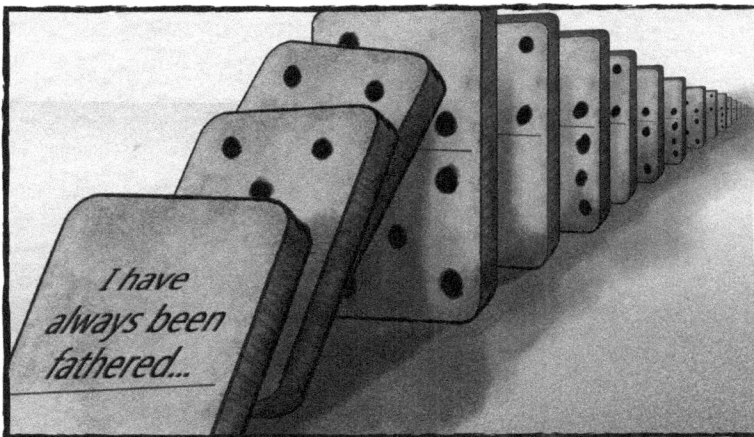

PALLIATIVE CARE

It was the phone call I was dreading for several months. The appointment of the death for a loved one often comes too early. Dad had been battling chronic pain for several years. After countless tests, there was still confusion among the doctors and specialists to fully understand the source of Dad's illness.

For over twenty years Dad had been suffering Post-Polio Syndrome (PPS), the cruel aftermath of his encounter with the insidious virus as a seventeen-year-old during the worldwide polio epidemic in the 1940s.

As the months passed by, Mum phoned me to say Dad had been diagnosed with prostate cancer and there was the possibility that cancer had spread to other parts of his already frail body.

Since Dad retired prematurely from pastoral ministry because of debilitating health issues, they relocated to Nowra, about 160km south of Sydney. It takes about seven hours of flying and driving to travel from Perth to Nowra.

I had made a couple of visits to see Dad at home, and each time I was confronted with the impact of this menacing disease. Dad has never looked so weak and vulnerable.

As Dad's condition deteriorated, he was transferred to Karinya Palliative Care Unit in Berry, just 17km north of Nowra. Providentially, my youngest sister Annie worked at Karinya as a palliative care nurse, and that was a source of immense comfort.

While Dad was residing at the hospice, I rang him on several occasions, and he openly spoke about his health, faith, and readiness to die. In April 2013, after a conference in Sydney, I drove down to the hospice to see Dad, possibly for the last time. I stayed with Mum and visited Dad several times. Each visit was strenuous and confronting. We enjoyed time together, talking about cherished family memories, reading his favourite Psalms, and sharing Communion (the Lord's Supper) together.

It became more apparent that Dad was also becoming increasingly confused and agitated. Had he developed dementia, or had cancer travelled to his brain? I remember one time Dad wanted me to take him home because of a conspiracy concerning the staff. I did my best to listen lovingly and reassure Dad he was in the best place and receiving the best help to manage his pain.

For the past twenty-seven years, my vocation has been a pastor of a church. Over the years, I have journeyed with many people through sickness, disease and even death. But here I am with Dad, not as a "professional pastor," but solely as his beloved son. I was daily confronted with Dad's physical weakness, yet in many ways, that was overshadowed by the strength of his unshakable faith in Jesus.

Then the time came for my last visit with Dad at the hospice before I drove to the Sydney airport to fly home to Perth. This is it. Mum was with me, and we spent about an hour together in the lounge that overlooked a lush paddock and the South Coast railway line. I prayed over Dad for the last time and told him I loved him.

He was apparently unaware of what my departure meant. Mum told me the following day that when I left, Dad said he felt sad, but didn't know why. Mum told him that when I left the hospice, we wouldn't see each other again until we were reunited in Heaven.

I sat in the car in the hospice car park for several minutes feeling utterly bewildered. It was surreal. I wanted to go back one more time to say goodbye, but that wouldn't be fair for Dad. So, before the long drive to Sydney airport, I rang Karen. As soon as she answered the phone and asked how I was doing, I broke down crying uncontrollably. Dad was only twenty metres away, and I was about to leave him. I was overwhelmed with the sense of finality.

A couple of weeks passed, and Dad's condition continued to deteriorate, yet he was bravely hanging on. It came to the point I knew I needed to book a flight to Sydney for his inevitable funeral.

As I was flying back to Sydney, I was astonished that Dad was still alive. I was either going to see him one last time, or I would be helping my mum, and my three sisters plan his funeral upon my arrival.

THE QUIET ROOM

I arrived in Sydney after the red-eye (midnight) flight from Perth and picked up my sister Ellie in a rental car from the International Terminal. Ellie had flown in from Los Angeles. We were driving down to Nowra, and neither of us had received a text informing us that Dad died overnight. We knew we were possibly entering a miracle—we were both going to see Dad one last time.

We arrived at the hospice and took a deep breath as we walked into the "Quiet Room." It was a beautiful single bedroom for patients who only had a few days or hours to live. There was a colourful stained-glass window of Australian fauna and flora above the bed. Before us was our dad lying in bed, sleeping and breathing uneasily.

Ellie hadn't seen Dad for a couple of months, so it was especially confronting for her. Like many terminal cancer sufferers, Dad had lost considerable weight, his skin was discoloured, and his face was gaunt.

The five of us were standing around Dad's bed amazed we were there together, the six of us for one last time.

RAISED IN POWER

After about an hour in the Quiet Room, Mum decided to go home for a break. Mum had been Dad's primary caregiver for over two years, and she was emotionally and physically exhausted. So, I drove her home and thought it would be good to get a couple of hours of sleep.

We knew we were going to be in for a long and distressing day.

It was one of those moments you never forget. Mum woke me up after a couple of hours sleep and said Dad had just died. At first, I didn't comprehend where I was and did my best to absorb the news.

Evidently, while Ellie was gently holding Dad's hand, she noticed his breathing suddenly became faint and peacefully stopped. Dad was with Jesus.

The five of us gathered around Dad's bed, and we knew that he was finally at peace. We were staring at Dad's body and the very place he entered a new realm of eternity.

We cried together and again reinforced how astonishing it was for Ellie and me to be present. The two of us are forever grateful that Sue and Annie, who live relatively close to Nowra, offered invaluable support to Mum and Dad in our absence.

This was a sacred time we would never get again, to honour Dad as his temporary physical body was lying before us. We held hands, and I prayed over Dad on behalf of my mum and sisters. I declared over Dad's body that what was sown in weakness was now raised in power.

Ironically, Dad died on Mother's Day, 12th May 2013.

GOODBYE DAD

The funeral for Dad was held on Wednesday 15th May 2013. All five of us spoke, and together we beautifully honoured a broken, yet remarkable husband, father, and pastor. During the DVD tribute that captured Dad's life with memorable pictures was the backing track of Hillsong's classic worship song Cornerstone.

Christ alone; cornerstone
Weak made strong; in the Saviour's love
Through the storm, He is Lord
Lord of all.

© Cornerstone, Hillsong Worship 2013

The anointed phrase, "weak made strong; in the Saviour's love" was a brilliant testimony of what Dad experienced throughout his burdensome faith pilgrimage. Through the unfailing love of Jesus, the weak are profoundly and miraculously made strong.

As I bring closure to my journey with my dad, the big idea is shame and weakness did not have the last word. When Dad breathed his last breath, decades of turmoil was finally and eternally silenced.

All the pain of Dad's shame and weakness that was manifested in depression, polio, regret, unemployment, chronic fatigue, and bitter disappointment in ministry had been once and for all silenced by the power of the resurrection.

Even today, as I ponder my relationship with Dad, there is thankfully no resentment or bitterness. When I think of Dad, I only have loving affection and heartfelt admiration. It has indeed been a pathway of grace.

In loving memory of my beloved father,
Kenneth Albert Mason
1934–2013

FURTHER THOUGHT AND CONTEMPLATION

Spend a few minutes pondering these words from American poet and political activist Denise Levertov:

"Every step an arrival."

What is your next step on your journey of overcoming shame and your mental health struggles? _____
_____
_____
_____

EPILOGUE

"Before the truth sets you free, it tends to make
you miserable." —**Richard Rohr**

Before we embarked on another family holiday to Bali in July 2018, something unexpected and disturbing happened. The plan was for me to go to Bali ahead of my family and spend a few days alone surfing, reading, and putting the finishing touches on this book. As a passionate introvert, the thought of time alone in Bali was pure gold.

Thirty minutes before the taxi arrived, Karen asked me an innocent question—"Are you ready for a few days alone in Bali?" Disappointingly, for the past several hours, that old and familiar emotion of intense anxiety raised its ugly head with a vengeance.

For a couple of minutes, I sobbed uncontrollably, and with humiliation, I confessed to Karen that I was terrified of flying and being alone in Bali. If I'm honest, for the first time in a long time I also felt the suffocating stranglehold of shame.

After a considerable respite, Amy (my amygdala) was once again on high alert; it felt like a replay of the Gold Coast holiday back in 2010. I honestly thought debilitating panic attacks were once and for all behind me.

Unfortunately, Bali 2018 wasn't the holiday I was anticipating and desiring. As in the past, the things that were enjoyable and refreshing such as surfing, running on the beach, and eating out, were once again a constant source of unbearable anxiety.

What does that mean? Just like in 2010, I needed to seek professional advice and go back on anti-anxiety medication. This isn't exactly how you should finish a book on shame and mental health—or is it?

As I said previously, I haven't arrived, I'm still vulnerable to anxiety, and I'm still on a journey of recovery. I believe wholeheartedly in the supernatural—I believe God can miraculously heal my debilitating anxiety disorder. Over the past several years, people of faith have kindly prayed for me, and I too have fervently prayed for a powerful touch of God.

Nevertheless, I also have another set of convictions— God is not only God of my ensuing healing; God is also God of my current brokenness. There is something mysteriously miraculous in healing that is distressingly unhurried. Sometimes the miracle is in the journey.

There is an anointing available and accessible for being patient and persevering, despite living with unanswered questions and perceived unanswered prayers. Today, I embrace the reality that God is wholly present in the here and now, whether I am healed immediately or not.

God can and is astonishingly redeeming what has been lost through living with shame and chronic anxiety. For example, my pain is now my platform—my weak spot is now my sweet spot. I can be an uplifting voice for people who haven't experienced instant healing and recovery. My story offers a fresh perspective on emotional healing and steadfast hope.

Shame and pain is not my identity or destiny. Shame no longer rules and ruins my life. I am determined not to allow shame to have the last word.

Allow me to close this book with these words of renewed possibility:

1. **Shame is a voice.** Today, allow God's unfailing love and reckless mercy speak profoundly into your soul.

2. **Shame is an assessment.** Today, allow God to offer you a new life-giving assessment about your current brokenness and future.

3. **Shame is a narrative.** Today, allow God to re-write your script from a shame narrative into a remarkable and transformational grace narrative.

4. **Shame is a weight.** Today, experience the weight of God's glory and rest in His "unforced rhythms" of grace.

5. **Shame is a posture.** Today, stand with a posture of resolute confidence, joy, and resilience.

6. **Shame is a thief.** Today, allow God to generously deposit His unlimited and unrestrained goodness into the vault of your heart.

7. **Shame is a connection.** Today, allow God to leverage your brokenness so you can connect authentically and compassionately with other broken people.

8. **Shame is a pathway.** Today, allow God to guide you along an unfamiliar path that leads to deeper growth and spirituality.

CAST AWAY

Imagine you invite shame with you on an adventure. You meet shame at the marina and hire a small boat. Shame is thrilled that the two of you finally have some quality time alone together.

You set out to sea and, after about an hour, shame irritably asks, "Are we there yet?" However, you remain silent and serene. After a couple of hours, the two of you finally arrive safely on a deserted tropical island.

You explain to shame that you are going to play a game of hide-and-seek. You tell shame to count to fifty while you find an obscure place to hide. Amusingly, you hear shame cooperate and begin to count, "1, 2, 3, 4, 5…"

Meanwhile, you quietly get back in the boat and leave shame alone on the island. You then hear shame shout enthusiastically, "…48, 49, 50! Ready or not, here I come!"

A few minutes pass, and you can hear a distant sound from the island, "Where are you?" Moment by moment the voice of shame is getting quieter and quieter—"Where are you? Where are you? Where are you?" And then there is complete silence.

You slowly make your way back to the marina with a smile on your face. You quietly and yet fervently say to yourself, *Good riddance shame... Shame off me!*

Shame is no longer a nagging and demanding passenger that once hijacked and derailed your life.

Shame is no longer tormenting you and consuming your life. For the first time in a long time, you are free.

As the curtain of this book closes, I leave you these parting life-giving words:

SHAME OFF YOU!

MOOD BOOSTERS

The following is a list of numerous approaches to help improve your mood. You will notice references to several "spiritual disciplines." Although the primary purpose of spiritual disciplines is not to boost your mood, by the gracious providence of God they significantly benefit your wellbeing.

Breathing
Belly breathing can slow down your heart rate, lower your blood pressure, improve concentration, and remove toxins from your body. See pages 71-73 for effective breathing exercises.

Coffee
Good quality coffee (toxin free) is a brilliant antioxidant and can stimulate fat loss.

Indulge in just two cups per day—early morning and early afternoon. Consuming caffeine after 2 P.M. can negatively impact your sleep. Of note, caffeine is not advised if you are struggling with anxiety and panic attacks.

Cold water therapy
Cold water triggers a flood of mood-boosting neurotransmitters and can also increase your tolerance to stress.

Gradually turn off the hot water during the last thirty to sixty seconds of your morning shower. Ensure you also practice deep belly breathing.

Community

The Church is a therapeutic community of faith, hope, and love. Belonging to a church is profoundly helpful for your wellbeing and the wellbeing of others.

Food

Over 80 per cent of serotonin (a natural anti-depressant) is produced in the gut or gastrointestinal tract. The gut is often called our second brain. A healthy gut is a key to healthy wellbeing. You are not what you eat; you are what you absorb.

"Leaky gut" or intestinal permeability occurs when un-digested food and toxins leak from the intestines into your bloodstream, triggering inflammation and an immune re-action.

Eliminate and avoid inflammatory foods such as gluten, processed meat, MSG, and dairy.

Eliminate or dramatically reduce sugar, caffeine, and al-cohol.

Eat whole foods and a variety of vegetables.

Gratitude

Daily activate the positive emotion of gratitude. For several minutes ponder one thing you are grateful for while breath-ing deeply and slowly.

You may find it helpful to write down the "one thing" in your journal at the end of every day.

Hobbies

Read a book, watch a movie, play a musical instrument, en-joy the garden, own a pet, learn a new language, play cards, or complete a jigsaw puzzle or crossword. Together they en-rich your life, relieve stress, improve focus, and boost your immune system.

Hot bath
Before going to bed, add magnesium flakes or Epsom salts to your bath to boost growth hormones and melatonin.

Laughter
Laughter is medicine for your soul [Proverbs 17:22]; as it releases endorphins, boosts the immune system, and can alleviate mild depression.

Massage
Through the power of touch, massage therapy can reduce the stress hormone cortisol and release mood-enhancing hormones such as dopamine and serotonin.

Meditation
During meditation, you access inner calm and rest. Effective meditation lowers blood pressure and releases serotonin, dopamine, and melatonin. Meditation in the morning enhances deep sleep at night.

Meditation is not just for Zen Buddhists, monks or mystics. You don't have to go to a church building, shrine, or monastery to meditate. You can all learn to meditate at any time, in any place, and any situation.

To meditate is to slow down, chew, ponder, and focus on Scripture, or an inspirational phrase.

Examples:

- "Oh, taste and see that the LORD is good!" [Psalm 34:8, ESV]

- "As the deer pants for streams of water, so my soul pants for You, my God." [Psalm 42:1]

- "Fear not, for I have redeemed you; I have called you by name, you are mine." [Isaiah 43:1, ESV]

- "And God raised us up with Christ and seated us with Him in the heavenly realms in Christ Jesus..." [Ephesians 2:6]

- "Cast all your anxiety on Him because He cares for you." [1 Peter 5: 7]

- "See what great love the Father has lavished on us, that we should be called children of God! And that is what we are!" [1 John 3:1]

Movement
Regular movement improves blood circulation, metabolism, immunity, and sleep quality. Active movement is a natural antidepressant. As the saying goes, "If you're in a bad mood—move."

Examples: run, walk, skip, jump, kick, throw, dance, box, lift, squat, climb, surf, and swim.

Music
Listening to relaxing music can lower your heart rate, blood pressure, and lift your mood. Create a song list for scheduled times of meditation and relaxation.

Prayer walk
Prayer is slowing down to connect intimately with God. Get outdoors, breathe deeply, walk, and pray. Recite ancient prayers, turn Scripture into prayer language, or pray in tongues [1 Corinthians 14:2, 4, 18].

Progressive relaxation
Change into something comfortable. Lie on the couch or bed and close your eyes. Focus on belly breathing for a few minutes.

Tense each muscle group for several seconds, then relax and slowly let go. Starting with your face, neck, and shoulders, slowly progress down your body to your toes. Don't rush this exercise. Focus on releasing all the tension in your body.

Serving
Think attentively about the needs of others and engage in random or deliberate acts of kindness.

Sex
Through physical intimacy, a chemical cascade of oxytocin (*love hormone*), serotonin, norepinephrine, and prolactin are released throughout the body. Collectively, they counter the effect of stress and help promote deep sleep.

Silence
Silence is transformational and ushers you into the "here and now." Through silence, you experience mysterious calmness and composure. Be still before God, to know God [Psalm 46:10].

Sleep
Good quality sleep decreases blood pressure and cholesterol levels while increasing serotonin levels.

Sunlight
Early morning sunlight increases vitamin D and serotonin levels, while improving metabolism, mood, and sleep quality.

Supplements
You only take supplements to supplement what you lack in your diet and body.

Examples:

- 5-HTP (avoid if taking anti-anxiety or anti-depression medication)
- Ashwagandha
- B-Complex vitamins (B6 & B12)
- Ketone
- Magnesium
- Zinc

Water
Dehydration can trigger headaches, irritability, and fatigue. The common question is, "How much water should I drink every day?"

There is no approved scientific formula. One guideline is to divide your weight by 30. So, if you are 60 kilos, you should drink at least 2 litres of water.

Increase your water intake during the warmer months, if you work outdoors or exercise, and if you are pregnant or breastfeeding.

Worship

Worship is surrender [Romans 12:1]. As you express God's worth; you are released from the selfie-life to sing, shout, serve, give, laugh, clap, dance, wave flags, play a musical instrument, lay face down, kneel, and raise your hands.

"Why are you cast down, O my soul,
and why are you in turmoil within me?
Hope in God; for I shall again praise Him..."

[Psalm 42:5, ESV]

SUICIDE HOTLINE

Asking for help is a sign of courage, not a sign of weakness. If you feel agitated and vulnerable while reading this book, please contact one of the following organisations:

Lifeline Australia: 13 11 14

Beyond Blue: 1300 224 636

Headspace: 1800 650 890

Mensline: 1300 789 978

Kids Helpline: 1800 551 800

RESOURCES

Act-Belong-Commit:
www.actbelongcommit.org.au

Beyond Blue: www.beyondblue.org.au

Black Dog Institute:
www.blackdoginstitute.org.au

E-Couch: www.ecouch.anu.edu.au

Livin: www.livin.org.au

Man therapy: www.mantherapy.org

Mental Health First Aid:
www.mhfa.com.au

Mindspot: www.mindspot.org.au

ReachOut: www.reachout.com

RUOK: www.ruok.org.au

BIBLIOGRAPHY

Amen, Dr. Daniel. *Change Your Brain Change Your Life.* Harmony Books, New York, 2015

Brown, Dr. Brené. *The Gifts of Imperfection.* Hazelden, Minnesota, 2010

Chatterjee, Dr. Rangan. *The 4 Pillar Plan.* Penguin Random House UK, 2018

Harris, Dr Russ. *The Happiness Trap.* Exisle Publishing Limited, Australia, 2007

Hart, Dr. Archibald D. *Adrenaline and Stress.* Dallas, TX: Word, 1995

Hart, Dr. Archibald D. *The Anxiety Cure.* Dallas, TX: Word, 1999

Hyman, Dr. Mark. *The UltraMind Solution.* Scribner, New York, 2010

Leaf, Dr. Caroline. *Switch on your Brain.* Baker Books, 2013

Meyer, Joyce. *Battlefield of the Mind.* Hodder & Stoughton Ltd, 1994

Ratey, Dr. John & Hagerman, Eric. *SPARK.* Little, Brown and Company, New York, 2013

www.ingramcontent.com/pod-product-compliance
Lightning Source LLC
Chambersburg PA
CBHW030933090426
42737CB00007B/416